D0595134

"Even though I consider myself to be a scientist, I find myself almost on a daily basis asking my patients what their heart is telling them. Finally, here is a book which can nurture them through the process of truly following their heart."
—Alice D. Domar, PhD, author of *Self-Nurture* and director of the Mind/Body Center for Women's Health at Boston IVF

"An uplifting book that serves as a reminder to reawaken the still, small voice within. Read it and you'll open your heart and mind to the divine and live a life you'll love."
—Lynn A. Robinson, author of *Divine Intuition*

"With both beauty and clarity Gail Harris teaches women how to find and then soar with the courageous voice of their own hearts. Superbly done."
—Paula D'Arcy, author of *Gift of the Red Bird* and *Song for Sarah*

"*Your Heart Knows the Answer* will transform your relationship with yourself and wisely free you into your more authentic self."
—Hannelore Hahn, founder of the International Women's Writing Guild

"Harris has written an easily accessible, practical guide to self healing and personal growth."
—Ellen S. Glazer, LICSW, author of *Experiencing Infertility*

"Einstein once said that we use only a small portion of our brain. According to Gail Harris, we tune into only a portion of our heart's wisdom. *Your Heart Knows the Answer* is a treasure map. Harris guides you to the precious loot just waiting for you in the nooks and crannies of your own imagery and intuition."
—Merle Bombardieri, LICSW and former clinical director of RESOLVE

Your
HEART
KNOWS
The
ANSWER

Your HEART KNOWS The ANSWER

How to Trust Yourself and
Make the Choices That Are Right for You

GAIL HARRIS

Inner Ocean Publishing
Maui, Hawai'i • San Francisco, California

Inner Ocean Publishing, Inc.
P.O. Box 1239
Makawao, Maui, HI 96768-1239
www.innerocean.com

Cover design by Nita Ybarra
Book design by Madonna Gauding

PUBLISHER CATALOGING-IN-PUBLICATION DATA

Harris, Gail.
Your heart knows the answer : how to trust yourself and make the choices that are right for you / Gail Harris. -- Maui, Hawaii : Inner Ocean, 2005.
p. ; cm.
Includes bibliographical references.
ISBN: 1-930722-46-X
1. Self-realization. 2. Self-actualization (Psychology) 3. Choice (Psychology) 4. Satisfaction. I. Title.
BF637.S4 H37 2005
158.1--dc22 0505

Printed in the United States of America on recycled paper
05 06 07 08 09 10 DATA 10 9 8 7 6 5 4 3 2 1

DISTRIBUTED BY PUBLISHER'S GROUP WEST
For information on promotions, bulk purchases, premiums, or educational use, please contact: 866.731.2216 or sales@innerocean.com.

*For **Bill,** your love allows me to continually discover who I really am and trust what my heart knows.*

*For **Lucas,** not that trust needs proof, but you're it, my precious angel!*

*For **Molly,** your heart knows the light you are.*

CONTENTS

*Are you getting tired of not listening
to what your heart knows?*

From My Heart to Yours

What is truth? A difficult question; but I have solved it for myself by saying that it is what the voice within tells you.

—Mahatma Gandhi

We didn't start out in life not trusting the truth of our hearts. As a little girl, I constantly sought the truth about who I was and why I was here. I knew that I was special, although not more special than the other kids I used to play with. It was a knowing in my heart that came and went. I never talked about it with anyone when I was growing up, because I wasn't even aware that I had it. It wasn't something I could measure or describe or see or quantify. Yet it was part of me—my truth about who I was.

My journey to rediscover the truth of my heart began when I became aware that I had lost it. My inner certainty that I was special, with something unique to contribute to the world (which is true of all of us), had slowly been replaced by an inner negative chatter that told me just the opposite—that I was ugly, stupid, unlovable, and fat. The chatter came and stayed for many reasons—my desire to be liked, social pressures, my reaction to my parents' divorce. Who knows? The reasons for its appearance aren't important. More important is that I believed it and therefore suffered a lot of emotional pain.

Fortunately, pain can also be a helpful messenger. When our body hurts, the pain usually signals us that something isn't physically right. My distress was signaling me that something wasn't *spiritually* right.

How could being *me* be so painful?

Somewhere deep inside I knew that I wasn't who those negative voices said I was—even though they were very convincing. Somehow I had never forgotten the special soul I had been as a child. As I struggled to fight the negative voices, they persisted just enough to prevent me from being the woman I knew I could be. This awareness—that there was a woman inside me whom I really liked and wanted to nurture—grew, until eventually I made a conscious decision not to live my life by those voices. I would live instead by the voice of my heart; I wanted this more than anything else in the world. Although the challenge was huge, I decided to take it on.

It seems the Universe never sends us anything we can't handle. Because of my decision, I was as prepared as I could possibly be for embracing the trauma I was about to experience. When I lost my twin girls prematurely twenty-two weeks into my perfect pregnancy—after almost five years of trying to become pregnant—those negative voices told me that it was my fault. "I told you not to jog when you're pregnant."

At this point, my choice was clear: I could either kill myself, or I could choose *not* to listen to those life-negating voices. So calling forth every last morsel of determination I had in me, I somehow found the courage to *listen to and trust* the voice of my heart as it welled up from within: "This was *not* your fault!!! What has happened is much too large for you to possibly understand right now! Have self-compassion, my love. Trust. Go to the depths of your grief, and you shall be free."

So I did. I forced myself to feel all of the shock, devastation, grief, disappointment, rage, fear, and utter despair, and then slowly picked up the pieces of my life. As I trusted in my process of healing (realizing, yet again, how those negative voices in my head have *no mercy*), my commitment to live according to the wisdom of my heart grew stronger still.

It became my life's quest. This quest, which I had begun in a less conscious way when I was a young girl, has offered me the gifts of becoming closer with my parents and brothers, living in a yoga ashram, getting divorced, becoming a successful advertising copywriter, owning my own business, remarrying happily, becoming a mother, and exploring who I am, as a woman and as a divine being of a higher power.

To find and reconnect with my feminine spirit, I participated in a weekend-long women's empowerment workshop. The evening that I came home from the experience, my heart was open and filled with love, and I sat down to meditate. During the meditation, the words "Your heart knows" came to me, along with a burst of energy rising up my spine.

Right then, I knew that those words had been given to me by the part of myself that wanted me to connect with my heart. The words helped me to see that my inner voice was an understanding of the heart, rather than of the mind, and that its qualities are consistent. They showed me that while the heart's messages may change, the voice itself is always loving, kind, and encouraging. It may get covered over by the other voices I have inside, but it is always present. It always has been and always will be.

That's when I began writing this book. I listened carefully to the different voices within me and studied their qualities and characteristics—their "truths." I saw the different parts of myself that spoke these voices, and heard what each of them said. I paid attention to how my body felt when the different voices spoke. I shared my experiences with other women and asked them to share theirs with me. I learned how to recognize the voice of my heart and to strengthen my ability to hear it. Above all, I found the courage to follow its wisdom.

During this process, it became clear that even though all my internal voices are seemingly part of me, the part that speaks "my truth" is my best, authentic self, and the part of me that speaks anything else isn't. This realization has enabled me to develop a much stronger relationship with my authentic self. Since then, I've taken a vow to "be" her, to live my life as her, to find her when I lose her—to always come home to her voice.

As I've learned to live according to what my heart knows, the quality of my life has improved dramatically. Things flow more easily. I'm more effective with everything I do, my attitude is much more positive, and I experience much more love and gratitude, because I know who I am. And now I can really appreciate the good times!

When I lost the twins, trusting my heart's wisdom became the saving grace of my healing. I became stronger as an individual, my resolve to be a mother grew tenfold, and my relationship with my husband deepened. I learned that living according to what my heart knows—even if what it knows hurts—puts me in balance, puts me in harmony with all that is. I have a sense of where I belong, a belonging in which I find comfort.

The journey to find the voice of our heart and trust its

messages is a universal human journey. I have chosen to write this book for women, because being a woman is such an integral part of who I am. However, the messages it contains—from learning to listen for what your heart knows to authentically living according to its wisdom—pertain to both men and women, so I invite you to share with the men in your life any part of the book that you think will benefit them.

Doing this deep and very personal work will enable us to find the gifts that we are meant to bring to the world— the gifts that will contribute toward making *it* whole.

Each of us has different gifts.

I hope that one of mine, this book, can help you discover or more fully explore your own true gifts. Most importantly, I hope this book will teach you how to listen to and trust the wisdom of your heart, so that you can live more authentically, and become more fully aligned with your divine potential.

The Way In

When heart chatter replaces mind chatter the power of love
flows with full force.

—Marianne Williamson

*M*y *heart knew that he wasn't right for me from day*
one. But I didn't listen. Four years later, he walked out on
me. How many times has *your* heart known something, but
you didn't listen, and then paid dearly for it later? How
many times has your heart known that a situation didn't
feel quite right, but you ignored it, and were very sorry
afterward?

One hundred times? One thousand times?

If you're anything like I used to be, try one million
times.

I used to live my life not trusting what my heart knew.
Instead I often believed what other people thought or said
about me. I believed the critical voices inside my own head
that said I was "no good" or "unlovable" or "a bad daughter," rather than trusting the truth of my heart.

Sadly, my heart also knows that I'm like so many
women.

We don't listen to what our hearts know.

Perhaps your heart knew that you deserved a promo-
tion, but you didn't trust yourself, and someone else got it

instead of you. Perhaps your heart knew that you should go to bed early and rest, but you stayed up past midnight anyway, and your cold developed into pneumonia. Perhaps your heart knew that you should have sprung for your dream house, even though the mortgage payments were more than you wanted to pay. But you didn't, and later regretted it. In this book I explain how you, too, can come home to the voice of your heart. You'll find a lifetime's worth of possible ways for discovering what your heart knows. I draw on examples from my own life and the lives of other women—the ups and downs, peak experiences and trouble spots. You'll read about pitfalls to avoid, opportunities for grace, and ways in which the language you use can help you connect with the voice of your heart. Your journey with *Your Heart Knows the Answer,* and the riches you receive, will be as sacred as you choose to make it.

Think of this book as your haven to come home to when you want to open your heart, come out of hiding, express your vulnerability, and find the still, silent place within. You can use it when you want to take a deeper look at something meaningful that's happening in your life, or when you simply want to frolic in your own authenticity and explore the nature of your own passionate heart.

If you feel uncomfortable when you're facing a challenge in your life, just keep in mind that the book can be most helpful to you then. Try not to push any difficult feelings away. Let them be. Having them is part of the growth process. When those resistant voices in your head flare up, just tell them, "Thank you for sharing"; then continue on. As author Sarah Ban Breathnach lovingly reminds us, *scared* is simply another way of spelling *sacred* when you switch the *a* and *c*.

Working with *Your Heart Knows the Answer* can be

especially powerful in times of transition and change. Like a lighthouse that guides a ship on a dark and rocky sea, your pen on the page as you practice the journaling exercises I describe will guide you through your personal dark nights. Morning always comes, even when you think it never will.

You can expect the way you experience life to change as you learn to listen for and then live according to your heart's wisdom. Sometimes change doesn't show up as we want it to. In other words, it doesn't always look and feel very pretty or acceptable at first—to ourselves or to others (it may never look acceptable to others).

So take good care of yourself, because new discoveries and emotions may leave you feeling open, raw, and vulnerable. Gently accept what your heart has shared with you, keeping in mind that acknowledging vulnerability is an act of strength. You don't have to get it all perfect today.

When you gain insight into yourself, keep this to yourself for a while. We must be cunning with our self-growth. By this I mean that it's best not to spill the beans about what you have learned to anyone before you have fully integrated it, because another person's negativity has the power to take your insight away from you. If you do choose to share your experience, make sure you're speaking to someone whose heart and spiritual inclinations are very much like yours.

Keep in mind, there is no *right* way to have your experience. There is only *your* way. Like a newborn baby who discovers the world around her by engaging with her surroundings, be open, without expectations, and I promise that you'll go far. For some of us, it may the first time that we are consciously connecting with this wise part of ourselves.

On the other hand, you may feel totally comfortable with your new discoveries—excited, exhilarated, thrilled, empowered, delighted. I've been there, too. Whatever happens for you (and it will probably be different each time you sit down with this book), be patient with yourself. Whether you're a pro or a newcomer to trusting yourself, you can use this book every day for the rest of your life to connect with your inner wisdom.

Above all, remember your intention. Think about why you chose to read *Your Heart Knows the Answer* in the first place. Know that you're exactly where you need to be, and that your heart's wisdom is your guide.

How to Work with *Your Heart Knows the Answer*

To help you on your way, I have divided the book into two parts. Part One explains how to distinguish the voice of your heart from the negative voices in your head, and invites you to claim the voice of your heart as the voice of the woman you *truly* are. Then the fun really begins. Part Two invites you to perform ceremonies and guided meditations that honor and celebrate this best part of you and help you cultivate and more deeply explore what your heart knows.

You will notice that I begin each chapter in Part One with a heart inspiration I received while working with this book. In Part Two, I begin each chapter with an inspirational quote that has touched me. You will also notice that each chapter ends with a section called "Delving Deeper," which helps you listen for—and hear—your heart's messages and incorporate into your life what you've learned in the chapter. It has three components: *Dialoguing with Your Heart, Your Prayer of Intention,* and finally *My Heart Knows Affirmations,* which I describe next.

Filling Your *Sacred Pages*

In order to do the important work of "Delving Deeper," I invite you to go out and buy a journal. For those of you who already keep a journal—these are *not* your everyday journaling pages. Whether or not you've ever kept a journal, you don't have to be a writer to gain a tremendous amount from working with these exercises. You can think of working with the components of your journal as filling *sacred pages*, a process whereby you will discover and honor who you *really* are and the wisdom you have inside. Whether your journal is fancy or plain, I guarantee that what you discover about yourself as you work through the book will make the pages divine. Before you begin the journal exercises, I suggest that you turn to the back of the book and read Appendix A, in which I describe how to get the most from working with each component.

Dialoguing with Your Heart is probably the most potent exercise you'll find to help you distinguish the "voice of your heart" from the "voices in your head." As you begin to master this dialoguing process—which you will— you can discover that the influence the "voices in your head" seem to hold over you is really just an illusion. Once you recognize the voices for what they are—other peoples' desires that you've internalized (societal conditioning from your parents, school, faith community, etc.)—they begin to lose their power over you. *Dialoguing with Your Heart* is a great spiritual workout.

Your Prayer of Intention helps you take what you've learned in the chapter and apply it to your life. As you grow more comfortable with setting intentions that foster inner awareness and spiritual growth, you can enjoy the confidence that achieving them brings, and your life will become richer, fuller, and more loving. In essence, you'll be in the process of discovering who you *really* are—a beautiful, unique, powerful woman—as you fulfill your divine potential in life.

My Heart Knows Affirmations offer the purest, simplest way to listen for and receive your heart's messages. You may start out using this process to work with this book, and come to discover that, indeed, it has become a way of life—that you are intuitively using it throughout the day without *thinking* about it—which, actually, is the point. You may begin to notice the "pull" or inner urge toward trusting the voice of your heart—which is your natural state.

Now imagine that you are standing at the top of your very own mountain, looking out at a beautiful vista, with a three-hundred-sixty-degree view. Before you, off in the distance, lie fulfillment, contentment, and joy such as you've never known. All your dreams and sacred lessons—experiences that will enable you to grow wiser, stronger, and more loving—hang suspended before your very eyes. Your heart yearns for what it sees.

Then a silver cloud appears, like a loving finger, beckoning you to move forward, to take that leap, to claim the experiences that your heart knows belong to you. Yet, even as the finger beckons, "Come," you know there are no guarantees. You stand on the mountaintop wondering what to do . . .

Then you realize that *your heart knows the answer . . .*

With that, I invite you to open to your experiences, jumping off from exactly where you are right now.

Part One

LISTENING FOR WHAT YOUR HEART KNOWS

Go to your bosom; Knock there and ask your heart what it doth know.

— Shakespeare

CHAPTER ONE

Whose Voices Are These, Anyway?

*Come to know what you know . . . not what you
know in your head, what you know in your heart . . .
Everything you need is right there waiting for you,
to own . . . and to give away . . . in love.*

A few years ago, I was in the hospital with a burst appendix. My dream of becoming a yoga teacher burst as well, because the month-long training program began the same day I was admitted to the hospital. Instead of doing yoga, I lay there with a gaping hole in my stomach. After my surgery, the doctors prescribed morphine. I was in a quandary. Although I needed the drug to numb the intense pain, it nauseated me to my core and caused me to halluci-nate. After three days of having morphine vapors spew out of every pore of my body, I knew that if I took one more drop of that vile stuff, I would die.

My mother visited me daily in the hospital. Even though she saw how sick the drug was making me, she thought I should continue to take it.

The doctors said so.

I knew my mother wanted the best for me. I also knew that at another time I would have listened to her and the doctors like a good little girl. I'd have negated my body's own wisdom and taken the morphine.

But this time was different. "Why," I thought, "should I listen to a bunch of doctors who don't care about any *inner sense* I have about my own body? Why don't I listen seriously to *myself?*"

I had one of the doctors prescribe a different painkiller, and my condition improved dramatically.

Thank goodness, after all those years of struggle and practice, I've gained a keener sense of my own voice of truth. I listen much less to that authoritative voice that is really the voice of others (my doctor, my parent, my teacher), the voice that tells me not to trust what I know and feel inside.

How I've loathed that voice—one of the many that speak to me every day.

You know the voices I'm talking about. There's the voice that tells you to get up in the morning, and the one that tells you to go to bed at night. The voice that says you should be happy, and the one that says you should be depressed. The voice that says you're attractive, and the one that insists you're fat and ugly. The voice that says you're stupid, and the one that says you're a gift of God. The voice that says you can't—and the voice that says you're unstoppable.

Not only are you filled with these voices, you run your life by them, as we all do. But whose voices are these, anyway? And where do their messages come from? A good friend once cautioned me on a cloudless day, "Take an umbrella. They said it was going to rain." Who is this proverbial *they* that she deferred to? That all of us defer to? And why do we treat the voice of "they" as if it were the voice of God?

Why is it that so many of us never question the "they" voice in our heads? We just listen and obey, like well-trained children. Some people actually live out their lives in this unquestioning manner. We need to look at the voice that keeps us distant from our truth, the critical voice that tries to keep us down by telling us that we're not good enough and that it's all our fault when things don't work out. You know the voice I mean, the one that says, "No, you can't do it, so don't even bother trying." The one that says, "You're too old" or "too untalented" or "too unsuccessful" or "not worth loving."

I'll use the term *ego* to describe the part of you who speaks this voice. Your *ego* is the part of you that *reacts* to the external world. It is the mediator between you and reality. It perceives the world around you and helps you adapt to your life circumstances. In that sense, it serves you well and comes in handy. But since the ego's sense of identity comes from an outside source, it's always worried about what other people are thinking.

"How do I look?"

"Did I say something stupid?"

Because its identity is externally based, the ego has fear and illusion at its center. It's the slippery fiend that at any given moment takes on *whatever* voice it needs to control your life—superwoman, bitch, victim, good girl. Your ego consists of all the voices that you've internalized and given power to. Since there are so many of them, I refer to them generically as the "voices in your head."

I used to see my ego as the "bad" part of myself, the part that got me in hot water and made me suffer. But my heart's wisdom has shown me that the ego isn't "bad." It just is. Like up and down or light and dark, the ego is simply one side of our being. Just as we couldn't know light if we didn't know dark, our ego helps us understand ourselves in relation to the world. Now, rather than using an "either/or" model with the ego as the "enemy," I see it as "both/and": Our ego enables us to survive, *and* its messages don't always lead us in the right direction.

You don't have to muzzle your ego—just don't let it run your life. As I've already mentioned, the ego voice is often our fearful voice. Yet, although our fears may not be based in reality, we must still have compassion for the part of ourselves that is frightened. This isn't easy to do. It takes courage to see our fears for what they are and listen to their concerns, without indulging them. That's exactly what we're doing when we listen to the voice of our hearts— we're being courageous and self-compassionate.

Discovering these kinds of differences for yourself will change your life. The game will be up. Those voices inside of you will no longer be vague, nameless entities that you can't pin down. You'll know them as distinct personalities, parts of yourself that you'll be able to recognize clearly. You'll have the choice of whether to listen—and to which one.

Indeed, recognizing which part of you is speaking will make it more difficult for you to keep avoiding the truth. You'll be too self-aware for that. And once you recognize the voice of your heart, you can't lose this recognition. There's no turning back. Once the inner light is on, you can't turn it off. Although you can ignore it for as long as you like, on some level, however slowly, its wisdom always seeps through.

We're all yearning to reconnect with what our hearts know. We long to connect with the truth we've carried around inside us since we were born—a truth we may have forgotten because we believed we had to in order to survive.

Isn't this true for you? Isn't your deepest desire to listen to the voice that guides you throughout your life with unconditional love? You know that voice as well. It's the voice I had enough sense to listen to in the hospital. The voice that led me to write this book. It's the voice whose power comes from within. This is the "voice of your heart." It's the voice that tells you that you're wonderful just as you are.

The voice of your heart has also been called the voice of your soul, the voice of God (or the Divine), intuition, the inner voice, multisensory perception, and so on. I will also use the term "the Universe" to refer to an all-knowing, divine presence or Creator of all. But please feel free to use your own term, be it God, the Buddha, a higher power, or "the Source."

The fact is that talking about our inner knowing isn't easy, because we don't have the language to do so. Indeed, language can only limit our expression of something that reaches far beyond words. For example, one woman I know told me that she experiences inner wisdom in her mind, not her heart. Yet, she recognizes the message as truth because she's always led in the right direction. So as you work with this book, think of the term "my heart knows" as a metaphor for inner wisdom.

Whose Voice Is the Voice of Your Heart?

The voice of your heart is spoken by that part of you I will now refer to as your "higher self." Think of your higher self as your best, authentic self or the part of you that always has your soul's divine potential in mind. Unlike your ego self, which is externally based, your higher self is the intuitive part of you. She's the essence of femininity and love.

Think of the relationship between the ego and the higher self like this: The higher self dons the ego so it can identify with society and fit in well enough to do its sacred work.

Sacred is the perfect word to characterize your higher self, because she's the free spirit inside of you, the inspired part that writes poetry, sings in the shower, dances, or expresses her creativity in other ways. She's the compassionate part of you that knows when to be silent, when to speak, and exactly which words to use. She knows who you are, how you love, and how you are both different from and very like every other woman you'll ever meet. She is that strong, unchanging place inside your soul that knows you are the source of your own power. She knows where you must go and what you must do to become aware of your wholeness.

In her moving autobiography, *The Story of My Life*, Helen Keller relates how she felt when her teacher Annie Sullivan took her hand for the very first time: "I was . . . held close in the arms of [someone] who had come to reveal all things to me."

Your higher self has come to reveal all things to you. *She's come to reveal what your heart knows.* It was *her* voice that led you to this book. Her voice speaks your deepest truth.

The kind of truth that I'm talking about is subjective truth, what "my truth" is for me and "your truth" is for you. No one can really know another person's truth, because no one can be another person. For example, no one can tell me that my experience of God is right or wrong or different from the way I experience it, just as no one can tell you about your beliefs. William James once said that truth is whatever works best to help individuals make sense of their existence. I believe that he is right.

My higher self, of course, inspired me to write *Your Heart Knows the Answer*—she's the part of me who wrote it.

The Connection to Your Higher Self

A golden strand that stems from your heart connects you to your higher self. Your higher self is a built-in mentor, best friend, and wise woman. Live in awareness of her, and you'll never be lonely or bored. Your soul will dance. Your feminine spirit will be strengthened and soar. As her words of love and wisdom bubble up out of your heart, you'll recognize them as the truth and act accordingly.

Sure, you'll be challenged. But your higher self wants these challenges—she *lives* for them and always has. She longs to live life fully and experience all of her feelings, all of the time—without necessarily acting on them. "I read and walked for miles at night along the beach, writing bad blank verse and searching endlessly for someone who would step out of the darkness and change my life," novelist Anna Quindlen confessed. "It never crossed my mind that that person could be me."

Just look at an infant. You'll see someone who follows her heart. Sure, the little angel needs care; she isn't developed enough to get on in the world physically, mentally, or emotionally without an adult watching over her. She also isn't lying in her crib thinking about whether or not she should reach for the mobile of butterflies flying above her face. She's not worrying ("If I grab them, will someone get angry with me?") or scheming ("I'll show them how good my muscle coordination is, and then they'll give me an extra bottle"). She just grabs the butterflies and gurgles with pleasure.

If we could only live our lives this way as grown women, we'd understand that the voice of our higher self, our heart's voice, never steers us wrong—even though we may think it is doing so at the time. The problem is that most of the time we listen to the voices in our heads rather than to the wisdom of our hearts.

Why?

Why would we listen to that critical, chiding, closed, controlling, defensive, authoritative part of ourselves that's out to stifle our growth, and whose motive often stems from fear? The answer is almost disappointingly simple: Even though all of us—men and women—possess an open, intuitive, feminine side, we are unfortunately taught from early childhood to drown out its voice and not trust it until we've forgotten that it exists at all.

Especially women. We've squelched our higher selves. Like Sleeping Beauty, our feminine essence lies dormant after the pinprick. Women are wired for hearing the voice of their hearts. We're wired neurologically as receivers, in tune with the nuances of voice, expression, sight, and sound, which register in our bodies as feelings and sensations (we'll take a look at the characteristics of these feelings and sensations in the next chapter). But we learned very early not to trust the messages we receive, so we stopped listening. And some of us never listened again.

Perhaps another reason we don't follow the voice of our heart is because it's hard to differentiate it from the voices in our head. Perhaps we don't even know that there *is* a difference—that we have these different voices within us to begin with.

Perhaps following the voice of our heart takes guts.

Indeed, following the voice of your heart would mean not only believing in your higher self but *acknowledging* that she exists. It would mean having faith in her ability to help you meet and overcome life's challenges. You'd probably have to take on some very scary propositions, like sticking up for yourself, believing in your dreams, taking risks, facing your fears. Stepping outside your comfort zone. Giving up illusions (about yourself and others) that keep you safe and shrunken. Embracing your feminine power.

How's that for a new way of being?

"Our task is to heal the internal split that tells us to override [our] feelings, and intuition . . . and have the courage to . . . listen to our inner wisdom," Maureen Murdock writes in *The Heroine's Journey*. She is right. Your higher self would settle for nothing less than *courage* if she had her way with you. She'd make sure you were living the life you were called to live, that your *every* dream would come true if it were aligned with your highest potential.

Imagine that. You'd have the relationships you longed for. You'd treat yourself like the Queen of Sheba—who knew her worth—and take delight as others treated you that way, too.

Listening for and living according to what your heart knows takes a lot more than guts. It takes determination. Self-discipline. Holding an intention.

And practice.

Although it gets easier to recognize the voice of your heart the more you hear it, you have to want it very much—you have to yearn for it. The pull to listen to others' voices is insidious and strong. Just as a ballet dancer must practice her pirouettes regularly, even if she's performing at the Metropolitan Opera House—*especially* if she's performing at the Met—you must intentionally *listen* for what your heart knows and then *live* according to its wisdom until this practice becomes second nature. And you must be able to do *both* if you want to live powerfully.

 Delving Deeper

Dialoguing with Your Heart

Your question or statement to your heart is, "Can I really learn to trust the wisdom of my heart?"

Your Prayer of Intention

Describe three steps that you will take this week to help yourself trust the wisdom of your heart.

My Heart Knows Affirmations

"My heart knows (*Fill in the blank*)." Repeat five times.

Chapter Two

Recognizing the Voice
of Your Heart

I speak only the truth,
My language knows no lies,
My words are as pure and as direct as sunlight.
I've come to show you that there's nothing to be
afraid of any longer . . .

*I*n this chapter, you'll learn how to *distinguish* the "voice of your heart" from the "voices in your head" and to *trust* that you know the difference.

How can you tell when your heart knows something? Let me count the ways, for they are numerous and very recognizable. The voice of your heart has many clear, distinct characteristics that differentiate it from the voices in your head. Since you may not be used to listening for what your heart knows, I'd like you to think of listening for it as a *skill*. It is the skill of *distinguishing* the voice of your heart (the voice that comes from your higher self) from the voices in your head (the voices that come from your ego). Think of *Your Heart Knows the Answer* as a guidebook for learning the "language" of the heart.

We'll be looking at these two kinds of voices (the voice of your heart and the other voices in the head) in relation to the following distinctions: intention; key words and phrases; guiding themes; physical sensations and feelings; and quality and tone of voice.

Intention

As your personal built-in coach and motivator, your higher self encourages and empowers you to shoot for your dreams and fulfill your life's potential. Without fail, her words, gently or not so gently, steer you back on course whenever you veer off—and we always veer off sometimes, because we're human. She wants nothing other than for you to recognize your magnificence. Her voice says, "You know you can do it!"

It also inspires you to join the PTA; volunteer at the hospital, church, or synagogue; or work for a candidate's political campaign. It inspired you to help that elderly woman carry her groceries home the other day. It has led you to perform these services, because it is the voice that gently urges you to temporarily put your own needs aside to help others.

Temporarily.

It also whispers in your ear, "Open that gift shop you've been dreaming of owning," or "Stay home with your children if that's what you want. You'll find a way to make it work financially. Trust."

By contrast, the voices in your head intend just the opposite for you. They will present whatever arguments or rationalizations they can to keep you down.

The voice of your heart carries your visions and ideals; it points the way you and the loving Universe intend your life to unfold. If you want to know whether or not to change jobs, or if you're thinking about moving to a different state and want some guidance, ask your heart. It will always lead you in the right direction.

What are the intentions of *your* inner voice and ego voice? If you can't recognize any from the past, don't worry. Just pay attention to them from now on. As you focus on these intentions, they should eventually become so clear to you that you'll be able to know instantly which voice you're hearing. When you do, write what you learn in your *sacred pages*. As you go through each section in this chapter, you may also want to write down what you notice about the characteristics of your own voices in your *sacred pages*.

Characteristics of Intention

Voice of your heart	*Voices in your head*
• Motivates, "coaches"	• Delay, procrastinate
• Mirrors your deepest desires	• Leave you feeling helpless, persecuted, victimized
• Asks you to stretch	• Tear down your confidence
• Inspires you to serve others	• Invoke fear and anxiety
• Never causes suffering to you or to others	• Keep you too busy
• Pushes you to discover who you truly are	• Keep your life chaotic

Key Words and Phrases

Whatever kind of situation you may find yourself in, difficult or easy, the voice of your heart will fill you with a sense of trust. It says exactly what you need to hear, the moment you need to hear it.

If you are anything like me, the voices in your head probably "should" you to death (i.e., they tell you that you *should* do this or *shouldn't* do that). "Don't Should on Me" reads a sign that hangs in my friend Mira's bathroom. Wouldn't it be great if we all had that sign hanging in our homes? Better yet, if we didn't need to have it—if we knew and trusted the voice of our heart.

The voices in your head fuel your emotions. In fact, getting lost in your emotions is sometimes just a clever way to avoid hearing the voice of your heart. Then you don't have to face what it is telling you. Josie's heart knew that she should break up with Tom—but then she'd be alone. Amy's heart knew that she didn't really want that second piece of cake, but she ate it anyway—and for two days afterward was bombarded by those horrid voices of recrimination.

Characteristics of Key Words and Phrases

Voice of your heart

- "Relax."

- "I love you."

- "Everything is OK, every-thing is right on course."

- "Have faith, trust."

- "You're doing great!"

- "Your beauty is like a flower in bloom."

Voices in your head

- "That's stupid."

- "Who do you think you are that you . . . ?"

- "You should/shouldn't, must/mustn't, ought to/ought not . . . "

- "Something's wrong!"

- "I can't deal with this."

- "If only . . . "

How about you? What dead-give-away phrases does your ego voice spout? What words does your heart often whisper in your ear? If none come to mind right now, pay close attention and you will see a pattern emerge. If you're not sure that you really can hear the voice of your heart, trust, and listen.

Guiding Themes

The voice of your heart has one job, and one job only: to remind you of your truth. Its guiding themes allow you to fulfill your divine potential in life. It reminds you that all your life experiences are designed to teach you something, even if, in the moment, you don't know what the lesson is. Your inner voice doesn't have to know "why."

Women commonly battle ego-based feelings of unworthiness, failure, the sense of being an impostor, and the need to understand "why." Did you ever have the experience of acing a test in school or of achieving great success in your career, yet feeling that your accomplishment resulted from luck and that, eventually, you would be "found out"? Did you ever feel deeply disappointed and frantic to know "why" things happened as they did, so that the next time you could make things turn out differently—so that you'd be in control? I have, many times in the past. So have too many other women.

I'm not saying that soul-searching and introspection aren't valuable. They are. But there's a big difference between wanting to better understand your life and desperately "needing" to understand. The former comes from the desire to know your own truth—what your heart knows; the latter from fear and the need to be in control.

In addition, the voices in your head keep you wishing for things, while discouraging you from taking action to make those wishes come true. This kind of inactive wishing is a true waste of your time and your energy.

Which of these guiding themes have you heard? As you listen to the voice of your heart, begin to pay attention to any recurring themes. Pay attention to any messages that recur in the voices in your head, as well.

Characteristics of Guiding Themes

Voice of your heart	*Voices in your head*
• You are a daughter of God.	• I'm a failure.
• Fulfill your divine potential.	• I'm an impostor, a con-artist.
• Everything that happens offers an opportunity for learning.	• I don't deserve . . .
• You don't have to know why. Trust.	• I wish/I wish I had . . .
• You are One with all that is.	• It will never work out.

Physical Sensations and Feelings

Hearing the voice of your heart leaves you feeling much more relaxed and calm than does hearing the voices in your head. You may experience an openness or an expansiveness from within—a feeling that you are one with the Universe. Or that anything is possible. (Your higher self certainly reminds you of this.) You may also experience a feeling of inner spiritual warmth and loving energy—a tingling within. Or perhaps you feel chills or a pulsing energy.

You may feel enthusiastic when you hear your inner voice: "World, watch me fly!" The root of the word *enthusiasm* is the Greek word *entheos*, which means "inspired by a god." So, if you hear the message "Take piano lessons," and you're inspired to run to the piano and start to play, you may want to begin looking for a good piano teacher.

By contrast, when your ego voice is speaking, what author Anne Lamott calls "bad mind kicking in," you may experience a kind of "blackness" or a "closing in." You might feel choked, as if someone has shut down your spirit's oxygen supply. Your stomach or facial muscles may tighten. You may also feel a pained look creeping across your face, the look of feeling like a failure. You might ache deep down inside, as if your very essence was being ignored or violated.

Listening to your critical voices can also make you feel panicky. You might notice your heart pounding. Or you may experience the opposite reaction—you may become lethargic, even depressed. You may feel as if you have to sleep. Your ego voice can wipe you out completely.

Now think about a time when you suddenly had an idea about something. Choose anything—an idea for a poem, a solution for a problem you were trying to solve, or the impulse to take a walk. Begin remembering: At the exact moment this idea entered your mind, when you had the flash, did you feel any physical sensations along with it? Did you feel energy moving inside your body, or a subtle burst of heat rising up your spine? Did you feel joy?

Two benchmarks of knowing true guidance are joy and relief. You can experience these qualities as physical sensations that bring delight, strength, or feelings of power. Look back and recall a time when you felt sheer delight— whether your heart was telling you to bake some cupcakes or to go for your master's degree. It's all the same.

Listening to your ego voice brings you the opposite kinds of feelings: disappointment, frustration, despair, betrayal. For example, when my friend Lauren's closest friend and yoga teacher suddenly died of a brain aneurysm at the age of fifty-two, Lauren was devastated. Grief-stricken. They had been inseparable, spending almost all their free time together. Lauren's teacher, who had a huge following of students and a local cable TV show, was in the prime of her life. Healthy as an ox. It was one of those tragic deaths that the mind can never understand.

Lauren was livid with God for taking her friend and spiritual mentor from her. Because she was so angry, she could no longer hear the voice of her heart. Instead she heard a voice that told her the Universe had betrayed her and that her friend's life had served no purpose. She believed that voice for about a year. But as she slowly began to open her heart and grieve, Lauren was finally able to hear the voice that helped her to appreciate the time she had had with her friend. This voice helped her, more than ever before, to value her friend's contributions to herself and the world.

It's impossible to hear your inner voice at the same time you are experiencing negative emotions—regret, guilt, shame, vengeance, jealousy, fear. It's like trying to remember the melody or words to a song when a different song is on the radio. The music and lyrics you're hearing prevent you from tapping into your memory. Your inner voice is strongest when you're feeling calm and centered. (Therefore, establishing a meditation practice can be very helpful for learning to hear the voice of your heart.)

Think about the times your inner voice and ego voice have spoken to you. Do you remember experiencing any physical sensations? What did you feel in your body when your inner voice told you something? What did you feel in your being? If you can't remember, concentrate on noticing the sensations and feelings from now on. Likewise, start paying attention to any physical sensations or feelings you experience when your ego voice speaks to you.

Characteristics of Physical Sensations and Feelings

Voice of your heart

- Calm, relaxation, joy
- Warm energy of love
- Energy rising up the spine— "the ping of truth"
- Feeling an idea being born
- Feeling like you're receiving an inner massage
- Feeling expansive

Voices in your head

- A blackness, a closing in, despair
- A pained, tightened feeling on your face
- A feeling of your spirit being hurt or crushed
- A panicky "I'm going to die" feeling
- Feeling lethargic, depressed, or sleepy
- Feeling dissatisfied, disappointed, or betrayed

Quality and Tone of Voice

The tone and quality of the voices may be easier for you to recognize than physical sensations and feelings. Connecting the two voices to their respective owners—your higher self and your ego self—is a great way to differentiate who's saying what. In a sense, what we are doing here is examining their personality traits.

Your ego, as I mentioned earlier, wears many hats. She's an "all-around-gal" who shows up in any way she can to get her point across: town-executioner, doormat, whore, glutton, and narcissist are just a few of her disguises. Choose a name for her that fits her best: "Baroness Von Victim." "Willamena Worrywort." "Ms. Snit." "Lady Woe Is Me." The more expressive, the better.

Many years ago, in reaction to an unhealthy relationship I was in, my ego self would often rear her head as an evil, miserable child. Oh, boy. When she came out to play, I often became passive-aggressive, sulking in the corner or giving out the "silent treatment." I gave her the name "Devil in Diapers." It was perfect. Once I had named her, all she had to do was sniffle, and I could smell her a hundred miles away.

Then there's Matilda. Matilda is my name for the part of me that used to eat compulsively when I felt emotionally starved, ungrounded, or not connected to my higher self. When I used to deprive myself of any sugary or rich foods for a long time, she just exploded, breaking into the cabinets and eating everything I'd tried for so long to avoid. After Matilda came out to play, those voices of recrimination would last for days. For years, I hated her for making me so miserable. I considered her the "bad" me.

However, I've come to recognize that Matilda represents the part of me that I deprive, both with food and in other ways (food is really just a symptom). Over the years I've made peace with her. I have a much healthier relationship with food and no longer deprive or starve myself. I nurture myself instead. In fact, I often invite Matilda to dine with me.

You'll find that naming the different voices in your head will make it much easier to distinguish *them* from the part of you that you want to express. Naming works miracles. After a while, you'll immediately be able to recognize the different "characters" your ego portrays, and you won't be fooled into believing that you have to play out their foolish roles. You can ask yourself, "Is this who I want to be?"—and choose who you are.

Let's look at the qualities individually:

The voice of your heart is always there.

As I said before, it's like turning on the radio. Quiet your mind, and you can tune in to its frequency. When you open up to the message, you'll get exactly what you need in the moment. Trust.

The voice of your heart is always in present time.

When you're bemoaning the past or worrying about the future, you can't hear your heart's wisdom. Being present is a *prerequisite*.

For example, suppose you were driving to a party and your higher self wanted to tell you, *"Turn left, now!"* You wouldn't be able to hear her message if you were obsessing about being bad at following directions or about meeting your friends when you arrived. Your ego voice keeps you out of the present moment, often by posing arguments or trying to convince you of something: "Now you did it, you screwed up the directions and you're already late."

The ego voices in your head wish and hope for things, a clever ploy that keeps you out of the present moment and unable to access the energy you need to pursue what you want.

The voice of your heart is direct and specific.

Strong and sure, it cuts to the quick, with "Marry Bob," or "Take that job," or "There's nothing for you to *do* now, just *be*." You may not always hear it at the moment you want to, but when you do, the message will be direct and unwavering. In contrast, your ego voice changes its mind all the time, one day telling you to go right and the next day left. It uses rationalizations such as "He's not *so* bad," or "Marry Bob, you're lucky to get him" to keep you disconnected from your heart. If the message seems to the point but is followed by a criticism ("You'll never do any better"), or it blames someone for something, you can be sure it is not the voice of your heart. Your ego doesn't care who it blames as long as it blames someone.

The voice of your heart speaks with unconditional love.

Your higher self loves you unconditionally (and loves you more than anyone else possibly can). She cherishes and adores you and always tells you how magnificent you are. (In fact, she's telling you this right now.) Even when she warns you of danger or prods you to make a different choice about something, her words are always loving and her guidance is pure.

With fear at their core, the voices in your head can be critical and bullying. Even abusive.

Cindy tells of an experience that perfectly shows the voices in her head at their undermining best. She said that one evening, just as her heart was suggesting, "Don't go out tonight, stay home," her ego intercepted the message on the forward pass and kicked it back with a new wrinkle: "Don't go out tonight, stay home, *asshole.*"

"At times like this," she said, "I see how my years of practice of listening to my inner voice have really paid off. In the past, I would, no doubt, have *become* the asshole." What a gift to be able to observe the culprit (her ego) in motion, yet not become it. Cindy's experience exemplifies the lengths the ego will go to trip us up. It also shows how recognizing the difference between the two voices can open up new choices for you.

The voice of your heart has a familiar quality.

The tone of your heart's messages is that of a close friend or family member. There's a comfortable, familiar ring to the words, an *I-knew-that* quality. A few years ago, I came down with mononucleosis—an unplanned two-month vacation from life, a plunge into the desert of bed sheets and Advil, with an occasional video when I found the energy to drive the car to the store to rent one. After a month, I had just enough energy to feel sorry for myself.

One morning lying in bed, after my "Woe is me" lament, I prayed, "How can I make it through the day without going crazy?" The answer came clear as a bell: "What would it take for you to nurture yourself today? Show me."

"Show me!" My higher self asked me to show her. So I did. Grateful for that nurturing request, I immediately lightened up and relaxed. I actually smiled, thinking, "Thank goodness, I only have mono. I could have an illness that's much more serious." Feelings of love and self-compassion swept over me. My whole attitude changed. No longer feeling sorry for myself, I had a newfound energy. I called up a close friend, Sarah, and told her how much I loved her. To top it off, it turned into a two-video day. I felt great—and grateful.

31

"What would it mean to nurture yourself today? Show me."

I printed those twelve words—in calligraphy—on beautiful rose-colored parchment and placed the paper in a glass frame with delicately carved flowers, which I can read from my desk as I write these words for you. They have become my mantra for health and well being.

The ego voices in your head can feel strange and jarring, as if you walked into the wrong wedding reception. Or they can feel *too* comfortable, as happens when you've been following their rotten advice for too long. For example, whenever Kristen realizes that she again did something she wish she hadn't, she says, "I'll have to slap myself around about that." Unfortunately, like many of us, she's comfortable with her feelings of low self-esteem. She believes that she deserves to be "slapped" around. How much more rewarding it is to risk self-compassion!

The voice of your heart is repetitive, consistent, and forceful.

Your heart repeats its message until you hear it (even if it takes a lifetime). Amy relates that when she first got the idea to sell children's books out of her home, the voices in her head said, "Who do you think *you* are, that you could run a successful business from home? You're no businesswoman." But her heart kept telling her, "You can do it," until she finally began to believe it. She describes her heart's message as "a consistent, forceful, yet loving nudge, like someone gently tugging at the sleeve of my soul."

Shirley, a woman who once lived in Boston, Massachusetts, consistently heard her inner voice say to her—after her fourteen-year marriage ended and she recovered from cancer—"Begin a new life in Albuquerque." Fortunately, one of the gifts that came out of this challenging time in her life was her yearning to listen more closely to the voice of her heart. Shirley followed the message, moved to Albuquerque—and loves it. The slower pace, the smell of roast chilies in the autumn air, and the beautiful terrain are all healing to her soul.

The voice of your heart is accepting, non-judgmental, and non-authoritative.

The difference between arrogance and low self-esteem is this: When the ego speaks in arrogance, it says you're better than other people; when it speaks from low self-esteem, it says you're worse. Either way, when the gavel strikes, your ego is wearing the robe—*and you lose.*

The ego voices in your head are childish and immature, like a bully who tries to feel better about himself by bossing another kid around. I admit it. I'm not proud of it, but I compare myself to others at times. I sometimes compare my body, my house, my husband. It doesn't matter what I am comparing. What matters is whether I pay attention to that voice, whether I listen to the answers. I used to. But now, when I catch myself comparing myself to others, I just tell my ego's voice to buzz off.

The voice of your heart never makes comparisons. Grounded in love and maturity, it has no need to "pull rank" on anyone. It finds the good in everything.

The voice of your heart is visionary, creative, and celebratory.

In a creative writing workshop I took at the International

Women's Writing Guild conference held every summer at Skidmore College in upstate New York, our first assignment was to write a paragraph about something that had deep meaning for us. Pensively, I wrote about my newfound appreciation for the *yin* and *yang* of life, for the existence of opposites. Next, we had to describe an inanimate object. I chose my engagement ring. Then the instructor asked us to write something that linked the two.

"Yeah, that'll be the day," I thought. "What do opposites like light and dark have to do with my engagement ring?" Later in the day when I was relaxing, my heart whispered these words to me: "The diamond shimmering in the light once was coal." Now I often repeat that inspiring phrase to remind myself that both the light and the dark are part of Creation.

The voice of your heart will speak to you all of a sudden.

Messages from the heart arrive out of the blue, when you're not thinking about anything in particular, or perhaps when your mind is clear after meditating. The message can be an inspiration (such as an idea that can help get a friend out of a jam), the first line of a poem, or the urge to cook your family a wonderful dinner: "I'll make risotto with fennel and spinach in a sun-dried tomato sauce!"

In contrast, the voices in your head are always calculated, based on what you were thinking about beforehand. For example, let's say that the idea to phone an old boyfriend whom you haven't spoken to in years suddenly popped into your head. If the message came from your ego, you could probably trace the idea back to something that happened earlier. Perhaps you had an argument with your current boyfriend and were looking for self-validation. But if the message came from your higher self, it would feel like a spark of inspiration and make you feel alive.

The voice of your heart never tells you that you are above or below anyone else.

Someone who is full of herself is not being guided by her inner voice—she is steeped in her ego. For example, suppose you were sitting in a traffic jam, waiting to get off the highway, when a large, cigar-smoking driver—neck dripping with gold chains—used the shoulder lane to cut in front of all the other cars. It would be hard not to call that driver a "selfish moron" (or something worse), wouldn't it? After all, he has looked and acted like one of those self-indulgent types who feel more important than everyone else.

"Selfish moron," however, would *not* be a message from your higher self. Sure, what the driver did was both annoying and inconsiderate. But your higher self would not have you put yourself above him by calling him names. She always looks for the win-win situation, one of love and equality. With a smile in her tone, she might instead encourage you to say a prayer for him, because he has obviously "lost his way." She also has a sense of humor.

The voice of your heart is an expression of your feminine nature.

Its messages are always trusting, healing, open, receiving, giving, accepting, and loving—the seven qualities of a successful relationship, according to the Family of Women, an organization that encourages women to empower their own lives. When you're not afraid of your strength or your vulnerability, and when you have the courage to love—yourself and others—you're following your inner voice.

The voice of your heart doesn't use reasoning or logic.

Lord knows we have enough logic in the world! What we need is more trust. Trusting our intuitive side, the truth of our heart, our inner awareness. Trusting that meaningful coincidences are, indeed, messages from the Universe. *That's* the voice of your heart. It doesn't use logic and reasoning. When you look at a beautiful sunset, you *feel* its beauty, don't you? You don't sit there reasoning that the sunset is beautiful. No discussion is necessary.

Once you *feel* the full beauty of the sunset, the chances are that your heart will become quiet. It speaks only when it has something of value to tell you. (If people listened to their hearts more often, there would be a lot more loving silence!) Immediate clarity—as opposed to convincing reasons and logical arguments—is one of the most recognizable qualities of the inner voice. And the quality we ignore most often.

In contrast, the voices in your head use logic to convince you that what they're saying is the truth: "If he cared about you, he would have called." When you hear reason upon reason, it's a good time to take a breath and reconnect with your heart. It might say something like, "He probably couldn't find a phone," or "What a wonderful opportunity to love yourself."

The voice of your heart speaks to you when you are open to hearing it.

Actually the voice of your heart is always speaking to you; you just may not be able to hear it. It may not come when you think it should or the way you expect it. And it won't come on demand. So if you are tense and are trying to hear an answer, you may not receive one. You may have to relax, so that you will be open to hearing it. It may come the next day or the next week in a conversation with a friend. Or in a newspaper article you read. You may have to take a walk or drive into town and, suddenly, you'll get your answer. All you had to do was surrender to the process.

What qualities of your inner voice and ego voice do you recognize? If you can't identify these from past experience, begin to notice them now as you go about your day.

Characteristics of Quality and Tone of Voice

Voice of your heart

- Is always there, never lost (you just have to tune in)

- Comes from unconditional love and a sense of universal lovingness

- Is repetitive, consistent, gently forceful, to the point

- Is accepting, non-judgmental, non-authoritative

- Is visionary, creative, celebratory, has sense of humor

Voices in your head

- Are abusive, critical, child-like, immature

- Are calculating, competitive

- Are wishful

- Have a convincing, argumentative tone

- Are negative, use blame

- Always have something to say

37

Whew! We just covered quite a lot. But don't worry about remembering it all from one reading. You're not supposed to. You can refer to this chapter as many times as you want, until everything in it finally becomes yours.

 Delving Deeper

Dialoguing with Your Heart

Your question or statement to your heart is: "How will I recognize your messages?"

Your Prayer of Intention

Describe three steps that you will take this week to help yourself distinguish the voice of your heart from the voices in your head.

My Heart Knows Affirmations

"My heart knows (*Fill in the blank*)." Repeat five times.

CHAPTER THREE

Deepening Your Awareness

Tell me, "Yes,"
Tell me that I can show you my world . . . our world . . .
The world inside your heart . . .
Your longing has brought us together again
To live eternally as One . . .

*I*n Chapter Two you learned the many ways to listen for and hear the voice of your heart. But there are other types of inner understanding that often accompany the voice of your heart, ways other than words (or in addition to words) by which your heart recognizes truth. As you become more sensitive to these, you may find that you receive insights in several ways at once. For example, you may simultaneously hear words and see an image in your head, while feeling a tingling sensation in your belly.

Why? Because some of us are *visually* oriented when it comes to recognizing what our heart knows. Some are *feeling* oriented, and some are *intuitively* oriented.

Pictures

You can "see" truth. Marjorie relates an experience she had working on-site at a client's office on a sweltering July day. Unfortunately, her desk was way across the room from a small, inefficient air conditioner. She said that she felt like a cranky wet noodle and remembers thinking, "How can I get my creative juices flowing?"

At that moment, an image flashed in her mind. She said she saw herself sitting on the floor on the side of the room nearer to the air conditioner, with her papers spread out all around her and ideas pouring out of her head like a waterfall. Then she heard the words, "Move over there." She immediately picked up all her papers and moved to the spot she had seen in her mind. She was so productive that the afternoon flew by. She said it was as if she had become a different person. And, in a way, she had.

Bodily Cues

Perhaps you're the type of person who is naturally *more* in tune with physical and emotional sensations when your heart knows something than you are hearing an inner message. For example, you may experience chills or a pulse of positive energy throughout your body without any accompanying words. Or you might experience a gnawing feeling in your belly.

Intuitive Knowing

You must have had the experience of *knowing* something without knowing *how* you knew. You just *knew*. Beth did. She says that on her very first date with her future husband she *knew* instantly, "This is it!" She says that if she had heard words, she would have dismissed them immediately. But she knew, without knowing *how* she knew, that that evening marked a turning point in her life.

Focusing on the Inner Dialogue

As cultivating awareness of and trust in your inner wisdom becomes your way of life (whichever mode of knowing comes most naturally to you), you will be discovering who you *really* are as you discover the voice of your heart. You will notice that the voice of your heart is direct and that its messages are based on a sense of acceptance and lovingness. You will begin to understand how the voices in your head hold a negative attitude and use arguments to get their point across. As you become more keenly aware of these differences, you may notice that these two voices can talk back and forth to one another.

Noticing when an "inner conversation" is taking place between the voice of your heart and the voices in your head gives you the freedom to choose which voice is speaking your truth. As you become better able to distinguish between the two voices, you will be able to choose more easily.

Dialogue Between the Voice of Your Heart and the Voices in Your Head

Voice of your heart	Voices in your head
• I'm tired. I think I'll take an hour's break.	• No breaks allowed. You must work the *full* eight hours.
• I'm going to call Sarah.	• Don't bother. She's probably not home.
• I'll tell Barbara the truth.	• It will ruin your chances. She'll lose respect for you.
• That ice cream looks delicious.	• You're going to get fat. You already *are* fat.
• Jan will love this gift.	• She wouldn't spend that much on you.
• I'm going to have a baby.	• No you're not. You're too old. You blew it.
• Bill will be home at around 8:00.	• He'd rather be out with the guys.
• What a great stereo.	• You can't afford it.
• I want to dance.	• You'll look like a fool.
• I'll write a poem.	• It'll take you forever.
• Everything is going to work out great.	• But, what if it doesn't?

Your Heart Knows versus Your Heart Wants

Using all of the information you have learned so far can put you in the habit of listening for what your heart knows and recognizing it when you hear it. But, as my friend Rosie once asked me, "Come on, Gail, when you're in the grip of emotion, when fear has you eating out of the palm of its hand, can you *really* tell the difference between the voice of your heart and the voices in your head?"

I had thought *Yes*. But I was wrong.

A while ago, I thought I heard my inner voice tell me that I was pregnant. Since having a child was something that I had wanted very much for a number of years, I also wanted very much to believe that the voice I had heard was the voice of my heart—that what I had heard was the truth. In fact, I wanted to believe it *so much* that somewhere inside of myself I made up my mind that it *was* true. In other words, my strong desire to be pregnant overrode my clarity without my realizing it. So, because I wanted a child so much, I interpreted my desire as the voice of truth.

In fact, not only did I think I heard the voice of my heart tell me I was pregnant, I thought I saw *signs* from the Universe as well. For example, we have a geranium that sits on our kitchen window sill. It hadn't bloomed in over five months, and suddenly—in the middle of December—it grew one flower, which I noticed the same day that I heard the voice. I chose to interpret it as a sign of pregnancy.

After learning that I wasn't pregnant, and after enough time had passed for me to recover from my disappointment, I realized that the voice I had heard was my ego voice expressing my intense desire. I saw how that *desire* had clouded my ability to know whether the message had truly come from my heart or whether it was just a very strong wish. In hindsight, I saw that I had been engaging in *reasoning* and *wishing*, two key qualities of the ego voice.

I've learned that when we want something very much, sometimes it's hard—or even impossible—to tell the difference between the voices in our heads and the voice of our heart. Because no matter how hard you may try to distinguish the voice that you're hearing, your desire may get in the way.

But don't lose heart. Think of the situation as an opportunity to learn something about yourself and about the Universe, and let it be. When you find yourself in a situation of wanting (or not wanting) something very much, think of it as an opportunity to trust. Your heart knows that sometimes it just *can't* know what the future will bring. Trust that the Universe has your best interest at heart and will reveal the truth to you with perfect timing.

 Delving Deeper

Dialoguing with Your Heart

Your question or statement to your heart is, "How can I trust that what you tell me is my truth?"

Your Prayer of Intention

Describe three steps that you will take this week to connect with your inner wisdom.

My Heart Knows Affirmations

"My heart knows (*Fill in the blank*)." Repeat five times.

CHAPTER FOUR

Meeting Your Higher Self

Celebrate the words that have you dancing
In the moonlight,
Embrace the voice that leads you
To where the nymphs do play.
Reveal a heart—yours—
That contains a universe of compassion.
Behold your divine, feminine ways.

*T*he voice of your heart is the voice of the goddess within you. It expresses who you really are—a goddess. In your utter humanity, you are a goddess—the goddess of YOU. You've heard her longings. You've felt her passions. You've longed to embrace her loving tones. If you told me otherwise, I wouldn't believe you.

Why? Because you're a woman. To love is a woman's innate gift and strength. Not only to love others, but to love *herself*—first, foremost, and always. (For how can she love others if she doesn't love herself?) When we understand that to love helps us learn about our power, that it *is* our power, we can begin to embrace the power we have within. The love in your heart is the power that matters.

Who is the powerful woman inside of *you*? What are your passions? What do you have to share with the world?

The sacred message of your heart is to become the magnificent woman that you know you truly are. Can you deny that calling? Can you put off acknowledging it even one more day? For the sake of all that is sacred, I pray not.

Embracing our higher selves as who we truly are is our heart's deepest desire. What else could our Creator have possibly intended for us, than to claim the nature of our own divinity? Could anything be more joyful? The reason you picked up this book is to embrace and express the wonderful, awesome woman you are—to know her, revere her, and claim her holiness (yes, holiness). To celebrate her, feel her vulnerability, to invoke her inner flame. To know the joy within her soul.

It's time to take a ride through your own heart's enchanted kingdom and know more fully who lives there. It's time to discover and express your compassion, your intuitive and receptive side, your power to heal yourself as well as to help heal others.

Yes, it's time to embrace a strength that you, as a woman, also possess. The Hindus call her Kali, this goddess of strength. Kali is the lioness who will care for her cubs with a loving tenderness yet kill anything in sight that threatens her young. Harness this inner power and you can accomplish anything.

Naming Your Higher Self

In the same way that naming the voices that belong to your ego self can help make those parts of yourself more recognizable, naming your higher self can help make her essence more real and concrete for you.

The name of my higher self is the "Czarina of Westboro." Because this name was inspired by guidance I received from a spiritual teacher, it seemed the perfect name for my higher self. But you don't have to have a spiritual teacher or have had any kind of spiritual experience in the past to give your higher self a name—that's just my particular situation.

When I'm aware of *being* the Czarina of Westboro, when I feel her essence within me, I feel more alive and connected to what I'm doing and to the world around me than when I don't—whether I'm playing the piano, writing, or washing dishes. Although you may find it hard to believe, when I *embrace* myself as the Czarina of Westboro, I trust that everything is right with the world—even in a crisis.

Why not honor your higher self with a name that best fits who she is, that carries her essence, her strength? Perhaps it's your own name, perhaps it isn't.

For your entire life you've probably been called by the name that your parents have given you. If you gave your higher self a name, what would *you* choose? Who are you as your best self? To whom will you call out when you need to be guided from within?

Your heart knows her name—go inside yourself and listen.

This isn't hard to do. Just close your eyes and begin to find that quiet space inside of you, and listen . . . listen for her name. It may come in a whisper or in a loud, clear voice. It may come now or it may come over the next few weeks. If you hold the intention to give your higher self a name, you'll discover what it is. Just keep listening. If you keep your higher self in your consciousness, she will lead you to what your heart knows.

Tips for Remembering Her Name

Once you give your higher self a name, it's important to keep the name in your awareness as you go about your day. Besides simply writing her name in your *sacred pages*, here are some tips to help you *remember* her name:

If you meditate regularly, use that time to say her name either aloud or silently.

If you don't meditate regularly, then pick a time during the day to acknowledge her by her name—*the same time every day*—such as when you're eating breakfast or right before you go to bed.

Write the name of your higher self on a piece of paper and tape the paper on your medicine cabinet, so that you see it every morning. Better yet, put reminders up all over your house—on the refrigerator, in your notebook or journal (if you keep one), on your computer. I call the hard drive of my computer "Czarina of Westboro," so her name is in front of me all day long. (At another time, "Czarina" was my secret code for access to my bank's ATM.)

Be resourceful. Use your imagination. The more you can bring the name of your higher self to your awareness, the easier it will become to connect with her spirit. *Remember to remember her name.*

Giving Your Higher Self a Symbol

If you're a visually oriented person or if you like to draw, you may also want to express the qualities of your higher self with a picture or symbol to help keep her essence in your awareness. Symbols are messages from your higher self. They are carriers of meaning that come from your imagination. Symbols work by entering your mind, which then interprets the symbol in its own special way. The meaning you give the symbol links your imaginative world with the concrete world. In this way the symbol has meaning in both worlds and therefore can serve as a bridge between you and your higher self.

A symbol can be simple or elaborate—a single stroke or a collage of colors. Whatever symbol calls to you is the right symbol for representing your higher self.

All of the goddesses you may have read about, as well as other powerful women from mythology, have sacred symbols. Aphrodite, Calliope, Athena, Isis—all have symbols that represent their unique essence. For example, Artemis, the virgin Greek goddess of the hunt, was known for her strength and integrity. Her symbol, not surprisingly, is a bow and arrow. The symbol for Pandora is a *pithos*, an ancient Greek jar for holding honey. This honey-jar reminds us to find the trust we carry in our hearts, even when the entire world seems against us.

The easiest way to invoke a symbol for your higher self is to sit quietly for just a moment or two. Invite your mind to bring forth an image, allowing the image to come freely and easily. The key is to issue an open invitation, without dictating to yourself what the image should be or when it should come. Don't censor what comes to you. You are bringing forth a new symbol, something you never before experienced in this way.

Think about it. Feel it. See how it affects you. Focus intensely on what arises from within and move into the essence of it. To shift into the essence of something, visualize what it is like to *be* it. Visualize and feel its shape, its texture, its other aspects. Then focus on basking in the light of its qualities. Remember, your symbol may arise now, or it may come just before you go to sleep, when you're relaxing or listening to music, or sitting in a car while someone else is driving on a long trip. Receive whatever symbol comes to you, whenever it comes and allow it to become a part of your life.

When you receive a symbol for your higher self, draw it in your *sacred pages*.

Celebrating Her into Your Life . . .

Congratulations. You just took two very important steps toward listening for what your heart knows by connecting with your higher self. You've given her a name and a symbol, or have begun the process of doing so. Appreciate yourself for the breadth of inner clarity you've cultivated.

At this point, you're probably feeling more connected with your higher self. So, now it's time to *formally* invite that self into your life—to stay! Surely, your heart knows that *this* is the reason you reached for this book. I hope you're up for the ride. For a ride it certainly will be—one that calls for strapping yourself into seatbelts both sacred and extraordinary.

Very soon, you'll call forth your higher self. You'll speak to her and allow her to speak to you. You can ask her anything you'd like to know. You've actually been doing this already—but may not have realized it—when you received messages from your heart.

Invoking your higher self doesn't mean that she'll actually appear before you physically. The idea is to invoke her presence within your heart, to feel her essence inside you, so that you can receive her messages. Whatever way she reveals herself to you is perfect. All it takes to invoke your higher self is an open heart and mind, some imagination, and the commitment to make your relationship with her a priority in your life.

But before we begin, stop to acknowledge that you've arrived at an auspicious moment. Take in the magnitude of the commitment you're about to make. Think about the events that have led you to this special place of union: love lost, love won, joys, sorrows, and searching; that undeniable, unquenchable thirst to *be the woman your heart has always known you to be.*

Feel the sanctity of what you're about to experience. You're about to formally acknowledge the existence of your higher self and allow her to become a more present, powerful force in your life. While knowing that she exists is one thing, formally acknowledging her presence is quite another. It's a ceremony. And, as you'll soon see, ceremony helps you experience the world of spirit in concrete, down-to-earth, bodily ways.

The Invocation

We'll begin with a short meditation to open your heart. Here are your instructions:

Make sure that you're seated in a comfortable position, with your back straight yet relaxed. Close your eyes and become aware of your chest going in and out as you breathe.

Acknowledge yourself for being exactly where you are in your life. Then, if you like, you can say this prayer of gratitude along with me:

O divine self within me, I have waited for this day to hear your every word. I have tasted your essence . . . dreamed your dreams. Come to me . . . and reveal the woman I truly am. I embrace you as the goddess within me. Come forth now in whatever loving way you choose . . . I will hear you in my heart and receive your message . . .

Now, listen for a message from your higher self, or notice what image she brings, and record these in your *sacred pages*.

If you didn't receive a message or an image from your higher self, you may have been a bit nervous or "in your head" about it, that's all. There's no hurry. You can try this exercise again at any time. Practice does make perfect.

Remember, this is the start of a new relationship, or the continuation of one that you're choosing to keep deepening for the rest of your life. What's most important is to have an open heart and mind. And to trust. You'll have plenty of opportunities to communicate directly with your higher self by practicing the ceremonies and meditations described in Part Two.

Taking the Inner Oath

Before this chapter comes to a close, I invite you to take one last simple step that will help bring you even closer to your higher self: I invite you to *take an inner oath to honor and follow her wisdom from this day forward.*

Taking this inner oath can help you connect more easily with the essence of your higher self and her messages. It can be a sacred act if done with intention and love—a ceremony. Before you take the oath, however, you must be clear about your intentions. Be aware of the commitment you'll be making—the commitment to *honor and respect what your heart knows from this day on—for the rest of your life*. And remember that you'll be making this commitment to no one *but* your higher self, and that you will have no one but your higher self to answer to.

Are you ready to take the inner oath? You've come this far—and not by accident. You've picked up this book. You've named your higher self and given her a symbol. You've even studied her language. There's no turning back now. This is your life we're talking about. This is not a trial run.

All you have to do is say the following inner oath, preferably out loud. If there's a different oath that you prefer to say to your higher self, write your own. That's fine, too.

When you can feel the essence of your higher self within your heart, when you know deep inside that you and she are one, take your oath.

Inner Oath

Dear (say the name of your higher self),
From this day forward—
I will feel your essence,
I will sing your songs,
You're everything that's true.
When I want to know my heart's potential,
I will always turn inward to you.

Whatever dreams you may have for your future, whatever visions you may be holding in your heart, *claim* your higher self; *follow* her voice, the voice of your heart; *be* that powerful part of you that knows you're perfect and whole exactly as you are. The greatest love story of your life—your *self-love* story—has only just begun.

Delving Deeper

Dialoguing with Your Heart

Your question or statement to your heart is, "Who is the magnificent woman inside of me?"

Your Prayer of Intention

Describe three steps that you will take this week to connect with your higher self.

My Heart Knows Affirmations

"My heart knows (*Fill in the blank).*" Repeat five times.

Part Two

LIVING ACCORDING TO
WHAT YOUR
HEART KNOWS

*There are no signposts in the sky to show a
[woman] has passed [this] way before.*

— Anne Morrow Lindbergh

CHAPTER FIVE

Ceremonies and Meditations— Practices for Going Deeper Still

The Promised land always lies on the other side of the wilderness.

—Havelock Ellis

*N*o doubt after working with this book thus far, you're beginning to discover that wisdom, *which is something that you possess*, is of the heart rather than of the mind. Perhaps, you're beginning to recognize this wisdom and trust it. Perhaps, by trusting, you're beginning to see who you really are, a truth that is here for you to discover as you continue working with this book, and throughout your lifetime. The process never ends.

The Ceremony and Meditation chapters that follow will give you the opportunity to practice what you've learned, to incorporate your newfound awareness and discoveries into your life. They will guide you to *live according to what your heart knows*. And to live this way as if your life depended on it.

It does.

Are you ready to accept an invitation from your higher self, to embrace your courage and deepen your trust? If so, then dance the dance of openness as you find your way. Your heart knows that there are no doors, and that wherever you are on your journey, you are always just beginning.

Working with the Ceremony and Meditation Chapters

The Ceremony and Meditation chapters could have been named the "celebration chapters," because as you work with each one, you will, in essence, be celebrating an aspect of yourself, a new awareness that is taking hold. So, rather than "thinking" about what you are experiencing, I invite you to *bask* in it. May your intention be serious and your heart be light.

Each chapter contains an introduction and a ceremony or guided meditation for you to perform. Think of each one as an "entryway to a different realm of your heart" where the waters may be deep and the rivers wide. By reading the introduction first, you'll know where it's best to swim and safest to cross. The introduction will set the context for performing the ceremony or meditation and may include stories that exemplify the issues at hand, as well as thought-provoking questions about such things as integrity and letting go of fear.

You don't have to do the Ceremony or Meditation chapters in any particular order. Bounce around. Read the Table of Contents and notice which chapter title or topic appeals to you the most on any given day. Try not to analyze—just go with what your heart knows. It will lead you to the perfect experience. Trust.

Ceremonies

Think of performing a ceremony as an act that helps you *make real* that which is in your heart and mind. It helps you become one with your higher self and what she longs for. It puts the power of the Universe . . . of trust . . . behind the things in life that you value most, allowing them to rise above the level of everyday life and into their true worth.

Ceremonies are extremely powerful, whether they involve saying a prayer, placing a wedding ring on your finger, or writing your burdens down on a piece of paper and then burning them. They acknowledge a positive force that's greater than your own—whatever you call that force—and evoke that force to come through you. So, for example, if you want to feel more self-love in your life, performing a ceremony that symbolizes self-love (see the *Self-Marriage* Ceremony in Chapter Six) will automatically open your heart to experiencing it. Think of performing a ceremony as acting out what you wish to be, as taking steps in that direction, as making your intention come to life.

Performing a marriage ceremony or reading the Torah is a sacred act because of the intention that underlies it. The intention of a ceremony is its purpose. Once you know the purpose of the ceremony, you focus on achieving it. In this way, ceremony helps you to use your will in reaching your goal. At the same time, you're allowing a higher power to support you. You're surrendering, you're letting go and trusting in the Divine. Ceremony, therefore, can teach you a lot about finding the delicate balance in life between will and surrender. Even the simplest ceremony, such as sitting in silence for a few minutes before you eat, can empower you and open you to all that life has to offer. Ceremony can help you surrender your ego and bring forth what is in your heart.

The ceremonies included here are easy to perform. Some of them will incorporate symbolic objects, all of which are things you can find around your house or easily buy. The most important thing to remember is to make sure that the ceremonies have meaning for YOU. Feel free to modify a ceremony in any way. Think of the ceremonies offered here as suggestions, and use all or any part of them to make the experience your own.

 ## How to Receive the Most from Your Experience

Read the entire ceremony or meditation through before you perform it.

Perform the ceremony or meditation in a comfortable place where you won't be disturbed. A room with soft light can create a sacred mood. You may want to have soft background music.

Before you begin, have ready whatever objects you'll need.

Avoid starting with preconceived ideas.

Begin by closing your eyes and coming into stillness for a minute or two.

Burn a candle. The candle's light signifies your desire to bring light—goodness, healing, and the presence of the Divine into your life.

Remember your intention.

TAKE YOUR TIME.

Breathe consciously.

Acknowledge what you are experiencing and where you are in your life.

Create your own personal altar. An altar is a sacred place where you display your ceremony objects or objects that have special meaning for you, such as pictures of your loved ones, something that connects you to nature, a gemstone, or a religious figure or symbol. Consciously placing the objects on your altar will reinforce your intention and open you to receiving more from your experience. Altars can be permanent, temporary, or portable. Place a cloth over the area you choose and place your sacred objects on top of it.

Guided Meditations

The guided meditations ask you to use your imagination in a variety of ways. They may call on you to focus on something, such as your body, as in the *Loving Body* Meditation (Chapter Nine). They may ask you to picture a specific image or story unfolding in your mind's eye, one that reveals important information about yourself. Or they may ask you not to think about anything specific at all, but instead to allow an image to enter your mind on its own (the kind of experience you had when you invoked your higher self and gave her a symbol).

They may help you relax, feel more peaceful, or heal an aspect of yourself that needs healing. They may call up emotions you wish to release, ease anxiety, inspire creativity, or provide guidance. You may be asked to pay attention to what you see, hear, feel, smell, and taste, since imagery includes perceptions that come though all of your senses, not only sight. Be aware that seeing with your mind's eye is different from seeing pictures in Technicolor with your outer eyes. Your inner eye sees differently than your outer eye. You may experience an "awareness" or a physical sensation that represents a message, a feeling, or an event. Whatever happens, relax and enjoy yourself.

The key is to *open up* to your experience. Invite your mind to present an image, rather than dictating to yourself what that image should be and when it should come. Ask or allow an image to come into your mind. Then be patient and wait. The image will come in its own sacred time. Remember, the more open you are, the more intimate and powerful your experience will be.

Don't be concerned if you're unable to see a visual image when you're asked to. As we already discussed, some of us are visually oriented; others of us are more auditory or touch oriented. Even if you can only think about or get a vague sense of what you were asked to visualize, trust your experience and let it guide you.

 Techniques for Guided Meditations

If you're performing the meditaton with a friend or group of women, appoint one person as a reader to guide the others through the experience.

If you're meditating alone, record the meditations slowly into a tape recorder and play it back *or*

Read through the entire meditation, and then recite your own version of the meditation *or*

Read through a bit of the meditation, relax and recite it, read a bit more, relax and recite it, and so on.

Engage in the Experience

When performing both the ceremonies and the meditations, try new approaches, play, take a light-hearted and receptive stance. Don't try to decide if your experience is bad or good. If you find that a particular ceremony or meditation triggers an emotional response, just feel the emotions, because they can teach you a lot about yourself. As you let go of judgment, you'll see that your body, mind, and spirit will feel freer and more responsive.

Be sure to *perform the ceremonies and meditations; don't just read them.* Even though on some days you may simply feel like reading a chapter and moving on, the difference between reading about and enacting a ceremony is like the difference between looking at a picture of your favorite meal and actually savoring it.

I can't stress this difference strongly enough. Sure, it's much easier and takes much less effort to simply browse through a chapter without engaging in it emotionally and psychically—especially if you're feeling some resistance to the topic at hand. But don't be a "browser," even if you're tempted. *Performing* the ceremony or meditation allows your learning to go much deeper. In fact, the more resistance you feel, the more you will benefit from performing it. If your resistance is very strong, invite another woman (or women) to share the experience with you.

In fact, try gathering a group of women together to perform these experiences. Although we may be conditioned to think that leaders of sacred experiences need formal training, anyone can lead a group in ceremony or guided meditation. "[In] the . . . spirit of woman's spirituality," author Joan Borysenko tells us, "every woman is a priestess."

Performing the ceremony or meditation as a group can add a whole new dimension to your experience. There's nothing more beautiful—and powerful—than women coming together with open hearts and minds to share a sacred intention. Believe me, if you find the courage to organize a *Your Heart Knows* group such as these, women will come. The need for spiritual community among us is growing stronger every day.

Keep in mind that you may feel the effects of performing the ceremony or meditation while you are performing it. Or you may not notice a change until days or weeks later.

Finally, if you're feeling a bit scared or intimidated, it's a perfect opportunity to tell those ego voices, "I understand, sweetie, now go sit in the corner," and to listen to the wisdom of your heart instead.

You're ready to go. May your experiences lead you home.

CHAPTER SIX

Honoring Yourself as a Powerful Woman

If we are not fully ourselves, truly in the present moment, we miss everything.

— Kabir

I've always loved the movie *The Wizard of Oz*. As a little girl I waited each year to see this enchanting tale that, without my realizing it, unlocked my own courage, wisdom, and heart. I recently watched the movie again with my two little nieces. As an adult, I finally—and fully—understood Dorothy when she said, "The next time I go looking for my heart's desire, I won't look any further than my own back yard. Because if it isn't there, I never really lost it to begin with."

I spent years looking for my heart's desire—to be loved—in other people's backyards. Throughout my late twenties and early thirties, I sought the approval of men, believing that if they loved me, then I was worth loving. I wasn't aware of choosing the very men who would reject me. I spent four years turning myself inside out for one particular man, trying to prove to him—but really to myself—that I was lovable.

Finally, something shifted inside of me that changed everything: I had had *enough* pain. I was finished loathing myself. I was *through*. Like a child who's filled with glee after being handed a cookie, I was filled with glee—after finally embracing what my heart had always known: *that I am fine exactly as I am.*

The real me was out of prison, and she rejoiced.

After that, something very interesting happened. I realized that *he* wasn't the right man for me (something my heart had also known) and I left him.

Although leaving was simple, it wasn't easy. Indeed, it took lots of courage, wisdom, and heart: the courage to face my own emptiness, the wisdom to know that my soul needed this process for my highest good, and the heart to allow myself to heal through self-love and compassion.

Not surprisingly, soon after I left, I realized that I could have as much fun with myself as I could with another person—perhaps even more. In the past, although I had often done things by myself and had a good time, most of the time I would have preferred being accompanied by a boyfriend.

I decided to put my realization to the test by planning a wonderful experience that I would enjoy all by my lonesome. Then my heart spoke these words: "If you *really* want to celebrate your magnificence, take a *self-honeymoon*. Marry yourself, then celebrate your commitment to love and honor yourself exactly as you are by having the time of your life."

Deep down, my heart knew that spending time alone in this sacred way was crucial if I was to heal my relationships with men. And most importantly, if I was to heal my relationship with myself.

So we set the date—me, myself, and I. That evening,

with Rimsky-Korsakov's *Scheherazade* playing in the background, I placed my favorite ring on my finger and married myself—right then and there in my living room. Then, dressed to kill in my favorite outfit, I cooked myself a wonderful seafood dinner. For after-dinner entertainment, I watched a Fred Astaire movie. Then, I danced around my tiny apartment. I hadn't had this much fun in ages!

The last thing I felt was lonely. Instead, I felt the Universe inside of me. I was alive, powerful, connected to everyone and everything. The evening had a surreal quality about it—as if I was having an out-of-body experience, where a million doors suddenly opened up inside my heart and outside in the real world, simply because I decided that I could walk through them.

I, however, wasn't surreal—I was more real with myself than I had ever been. Not surprisingly, I felt vulnerable, as if I had discovered a secret that was way too personal, too delicate, to share with anyone—yet. Still, I knew the doors had opened.

As a result of performing my self-marriage and taking my self-honeymoon, I realized that I had been looking for an intimate relationship with a partner without having been intimate with myself. "How can one be intimate with herself?" you may be asking. Usually, we think of intimacy as a quality that we share with others. But you can only recognize in another that which you see in yourself. So, the more fully you know yourself, the more fully you can know someone else.

We deny whole pieces of ourselves—foregoing self-intimacy—not only because we're afraid of our weaknesses and our vulnerabilities but because we're afraid of our power, we're afraid of success. We don't realize that by embracing our vulnerability we grow strong. How intimate are you with yourself? Which of your qualities do you own and value? Do you embrace your beauty? And what about the aspects of yourself that you're not so crazy about? Do you acknowledge them as well, or do you run from them, pretending that they don't exist?

Having an intimate relationship with yourself requires accepting more than just the parts of yourself that you like. It also requires that you look at and accept what psychotherapist Carl Jung called the *shadow* self. All of us have a shadow self. It is the side of ourselves that we deny or disown.

Your shadow self embodies the parts of you that were hurt or didn't mature and of which you are ashamed. The more you deny them, the stronger the force they will have upon your life. Your ego self finds myriad ways to keep you from acknowledging your shadow self, those aspects of yourself, for example, that are angry, filled with rage, lazy, or lustful. Your shadow self can also consist of more positive qualities that you may be hiding from, such as leadership, healthy sexuality, honesty, or the ability to give.

Your shadow's gift to you is the opportunity to become aware of your dark side, so that its power can be accessed and used in healthy ways, such as through your passions. Let your shadow become your friend.

In order to claim our wholeness, we must have the courage to acknowledge those parts of ourselves that we don't want to see, those parts from which we have split. Only then can we recognize their illusoriness, can we claim our true power and feel the joy that is of our soul.

Was there ever a time in your life when you were in your power—and you *knew* it? Perhaps, a time when you were in the limelight, alone in nature, or making love with someone special. If so, bring yourself back to that moment.

How did you feel about yourself? Was your heart open or closed? Was there anything that needed changing, or was everything perfect just as it was? Did you feel part of a larger whole?

Powerful moments such as these are available to you *every* time you choose to act on knowing who you really are—your higher self. Think about how many opportunities you have during the day to make empowered choices for yourself. Imagine what your life would be like if making them became a habit.

Here's a choice for you to make. Will you stand up and marry yourself today? Marrying yourself means that you're ready to say "I do" to yourself *exactly as you are.* You're ready to love, honor, and respect yourself—right now, this very moment—not after you remedy those few last flaws. You don't need any fixing.

However, be sure not to confuse "fixing" with growing. If you love and honor yourself, then you can't help but continue growing the rest of your life.

Why not choose to love yourself right now by joining me in performing the *Self-Marriage* Ceremony that follows. The *Self-Marriage* Ceremony is a joyous celebration of self-love and self-acceptance. Loving yourself exactly as you are—*faults and all* —is the key to being intimate with yourself and living as an empowered individual. Only *then* is it possible to have wonderfully intimate, satisfying relationships with others. Then, the world can truly be your oyster.

Don't be fooled. The *Self-Marriage* Ceremony is for all women, whether married, single, divorced, separated, soon to be separated, soon to be married, or in a partnership. It's for women who want to be married and women who want to remain single. It's for straight women and lesbians. All of us can benefit from stepping into our power more fully.

69

If you're not married but wish to be, consider this ceremony a pre-nuptial necessity. If you already are married or have a partner, it is an opportunity to experience a new and deeper love for yourself, which you can bring to your marriage or partnership for the rest of your life. If you choose not to be in a marriage or committed relationship, this ceremony will help you become more intimate with yourself, and have deeper, more intimate relationships with everyone in your life.

Although the *Self-Marriage* Ceremony takes just a few minutes to perform, its effect on your life can be profound, especially if you take your vows seriously.

It's time—bride-to-be—to prepare for your sacred self-marriage ceremony. I'll bring the rice.

The Self-Marriage Ceremony for Honoring Yourself as a Powerful Woman

Being a woman is a wonderful, mysterious, glorious adventure. Fall in love with yourself. Have a splendid relationship with You. Get intimate with yourself. Celebrate all the little (and big) things that make You magnificent. Rejoice in your own beauty.

In preparation for the *Self-Marriage* Ceremony, think about what you would like to wear as you take your vows. You may want to honor yourself with a gift after you complete the ceremony. Let your choices symbolize the self-love you have nurtured. The more personal and intimate you make your experience, the more you will derive from it.

The ceremony has four sequential parts: performing the ceremony, signing your Self-Marriage Certificate, taking your Self-Honeymoon, and living your Self-Marriage Vows, each an integral part of your experience.

You will need:

- A ring (any ring will do as long as it has special meaning for you)

- Your favorite outfit

- A mirror

- A candle

- A gift offering, something representing your inner worth

- A beautiful piece of paper

- A pretty colored magic marker

- A few free hours (for your self-honeymoon)

Part One

Performing the Self-Marriage Ceremony

Perform the ceremony in a comfortable setting, such as your bedroom or living room—and if possible, in front of a mirror. Watching yourself as you say your Self-Marriage vows can make the experience especially meaningful.

Directions:

1. Have ready all the articles that you'll need for the ceremony.

2. Close your eyes. Go to the place within that knows your deep sense of self. Bask in the calmness.

3. If you feel either resistance or anticipation, acknowledge it and gently let it go.

4. Honor all that you've done to prepare for this ceremony.

5. Light your candle.

6. Say your Self-Marriage Vows. Use the vows below as a reference, or if you prefer, create your own.

7. Place your ring on your finger.

8. *Let it all in.* After a few moments of inner silence, begin to feel the gift of joy and freedom that you have bestowed upon yourself.

The Self-Marriage Vows

I will always love, honor, and respect myself.
I am devoted to my growth.
I hold my life as sacred,
And loving relationships as food for my soul.
I will always seek the truth,
And never forsake myself.
Through thick and thin, I will love myself forever.

Part Two

Signing the Self-Marriage Certificate

After you say your Self-Marriage Vows, create and sign your Self-Marriage Certificate. Find some beautiful paper, use a gold or silver marker—whatever will make the certificate special for you. You can use the example below as inspiration. Signing your Self-Marriage Certificate reinforces the act of self-love you just initiated and enables you to cherish your vows more deeply.

Certificate of Self-Marriage

I, [fill in your name] hereby marry myself on this day of _____. I swear that from this day forward I will always come home to myself. I bestow upon myself self-love to last a lifetime.

Signed _____. Witnessed by my higher self [fill in name].

Part Three

The Self-Honeymoon

Now that you've taken your vows, it's time to start living them. Taking your Self-Honeymoon is your first opportunity—of many—to incorporate your Self-Marriage Vows into your life. It will allow you to celebrate yourself and your Self-Marriage in a way that can open up new doors for your soul.

Spend a few hours by yourself doing exactly what you love to do best. Find ways to nurture yourself: see a movie, go to a museum, take a walk, take a nap, sing, dance, go to the beach, go to Paris, cook, jog, stretch, paint—whatever gives you pleasure. Think of your Self-Honeymoon as an opportunity to party with yourself. Love, honor, and respect the beautiful woman that you are. And remember—there's no else one to please. So go have yourself a ball.

Part Four
Living the Self-Marriage Vows

It's important to "live" what you've gained from performing the Self-Marriage Ceremony. Incorporating the Self-Marriage Vows into your daily life is a great way to begin.

Memorize your vows. Memorizing them helps you place their meaning deep within your heart. Once you memorize your vows, you'll never feel lonely again for long.

Begin each day by silently reciting your vows. This will help you know who you really are and will help you open to love. If you ever feel a longing in your heart, feel empty, frightened, or disconnected from yourself, recite your vows again. Like a compass, they'll lead you back to your higher self.

In challenging times, recite your vows often. Doing so will support you in being strong and having the same compassion for yourself that you would for someone else in a similar situation. Repeating your vows often will help you remember that your life is sacred.

Delving Deeper

Dialoguing with Your Heart

Your question or statement to your heart is, "When I accept myself . . . "

Your Prayer of Intention

After performing the *Self-Marriage* Ceremony, describe three steps that you will take this week to practice self-love.

My Heart Knows Affirmations

"My heart knows (*Fill in the blank*)." Repeat five times.

CHAPTER SEVEN

Living the Full Life

It's a funny thing about life. If you refuse to settle for anything less than the best, that's what it will give you.

— W. Somerset Maugham

𝒜s you probably know, life is *not* always a bed of roses. We long for things we can't grab hold of—a great relationship, more money, peace of mind. Things befall us that we haven't quite bargained for—infertility, a miserable boss, a fire, the death of a loved one.

Although so much in life is out of our control, we often try to *hold on to* or *force* a situation rather than surrender to our own unique divine plan. However, as you are also probably quite well aware, holding on and forcing don't work. When a relationship is over, it's over; you can't get it back no matter how hard you pray.

Your heart knows.

The "Serenity Prayer," a beautiful, well-known invocation that is the motto for the Twelve-Step programs, most eloquently praises this heart wisdom. The prayer says, "God grant me the serenity to accept the things I cannot change, the courage to change the things I can, and the wisdom to know the difference."

I appreciate the part about knowing the difference. Because, yes, there's a lot we can't change—but a lot we can, if only we trust—in ourselves and in a power that's greater than we are. Where in your life do you not trust yourself? And why? I got the message early on that if I wanted *too* much for myself, I was being selfish. My translation of this message was that I don't *deserve* much. Was your experience similar to mine?

What does the word *selfish* mean, anyway? Webster's Dictionary defines it as: "deficient in consideration for others; concerned with one's own personal profit or pleasure; actuated by self-interest." But does caring for the self mean that one is selfish?

This question is a critical one for all women to ask— particularly for those of us who want to listen to the voices of our hearts. Perhaps we can be *perceived* as selfish if our needs conflict with someone else's but we attend first, or only, to our own. You may have come up against this kind of situation at some point with a family member or spouse.

Miriam came up against it when her ailing parents could no longer function on their own and needed to go into a nursing home. Several of her aunts, however, kept pressuring her to continue bearing the burden of caring for her parents, despite its disrupting the lives of her entire family. She felt very guilty and conflicted about what to do.

What was the right choice for Miriam? It all depended on who was choosing—her higher self or her ego self. "No one is hurt by doing the right thing," says a Hawaiian proverb. If Miriam had followed the voice of her heart, her decision to place her parents in the nursing home *couldn't* have been wrong for them, although other people might not have understood it at the time—or ever.

We don't live in a vacuum. We're all part of the web of life; our purposes and our energies fit together like a big jigsaw puzzle or divine mosaic. What's truly good for me *cannot* be bad for you. If you're unsure whether you're being selfish in a particular situation, ask yourself who is choosing—your higher self or your ego self. If your higher self is choosing, you're not being selfish.

But can *you* believe this? Have you played out the "selfish syndrome" as I have, believing that really wanting something for yourself makes you selfish? What do you want right now: More time to yourself? To lose twenty pounds? Those expensive shoes you've been eyeing for months? To quit corporate America and go out on your own? To be a stay-at-home mom?

And what stops you from attaining the things you want: Fear of failure? Fear of success? Believing that you don't deserve them?

Bingo.

Most of us just don't think we're damn worth it. Deep down, we don't think we *deserve* the things we want. But because painful feelings are difficult to carry around day after day, we tend to disguise them: by always being busy, by gaining weight, by numbing ourselves, by simply denying our deepest longings.

Could it be that in your heart of hearts you don't believe that you deserve the things you want?

The things we truly desire in life are, indeed, aligned with our divine potential. These include the big as well as the little things, from that marriage or primary relationship you've been longing for to that writing class you've wanted to take to that challenging conversation you've been finding the courage within yourself to initiate.

I'm not speaking about the things that you may *think* you want—but that are not aligned with your highest potential. I'm not talking about giving in to your emotions when your inner two-year-old is having a tantrum. I'm talking about the things *you know in your heart* belong to you. Living from the stance that you *deserve* what you desire draws to you that which you need for those desires to manifest—the right people, the right opportunities, the right timing.

You *do* deserve your heart's desires. Can you say that statement about yourself, three times—aloud? Think about something that your heart really wants. Then take a deep breath and say, "I deserve it. I deserve it. I deserve it."

Was this hard to do? Did you hesitate at all? If you did, something is getting in your way. That "something" may be unresolved feelings of low self-esteem or other feelings that you may have been carrying around, probably for a long, long time.

Finally, I believe that what stops us from knowing that we are worthy is that we believe we're separate from God (or any form of divinity). We believe that we're less than we really are—yet if God created us, we are a part of God.

We weren't born feeling unworthy. Did you ever see a baby with low self-esteem? Of course not. It's only after we learn to abide by society's rules, dictated to us by our parents, schools, faith communities, politicians, and the media that we forget who we really are and the power within us to manifest that which we want. Listen to your higher self— she'll tell you everything that you deserve. And the best news of all is that you have the rest of your life to agree with her and to act on her promptings.

It's time to rediscover the part of yourself that knows you deserve to have *everything* you truly wish for that's aligned with your divine potential in life. With that in mind, I invite you to join me in performing the *Rose Petal* Ceremony that follows. The *Rose Petal* Ceremony uses roses, but there's nothing else flowery about it.

The ceremony guides you to look within and discover those things or qualities in your life that belong to you if only you would claim them, so that you can declare—to yourself and to the world—that which is your birthright. It gives you practice in having courage as you take steps toward acting and receiving that which your heart truly yearns for—big and small. Once you become aware of what you truly yearn for, the right circumstances will arise to draw that very thing or quality to you.

That's powerful stuff. But I know you're up for it, or you wouldn't be reading these words. The *Rose Petal* Ceremony awaits you. Now, in celebration, go out and buy yourself a dozen long-stemmed roses.

The Rose Petal Ceremony for
Living the Full Life

Petals of desire,
Petals of Truth
Let your life blossom,
Let your life bloom
Your bed of roses
Lies just outside your window.
Open it wide.
See how sweet you can stand it.
See how sweet can you truly stand it.

In preparation for the *Rose Petal* Ceremony, begin to think about those things or qualities that you yearn for and have yet to experience. To gain the most from performing the ceremony, come up with as many ideas as you can. If this is difficult to do, it may be because you don't think that you deserve them. If so, ask yourself, "If I did desire new things in my life that enabled me to continue growing, what would they be?" Now, you are ready to perform the ceremony.

You will need:

- A beautiful bowl filled halfway with water

- Two voluptuous roses

- An open heart

Directions:

1. Peel a rose petal from one of the roses.

2. Place the petal in the bowl of water and state out loud something that you desire.

   Examples:

   Say: "I want (*to go to France*)."

   Say: "I want (*an intimate relationship*)."

   Say: "I want (*peace of mind*)."

3. Close your eyes and breathe for a few minutes. Keep breathing until you find that place deep inside yourself

that *knows* you deserve to have this thing. This knowledge can be felt strongly (as if it were fireworks) or softly (as if it were a dimly flickering candle). It doesn't matter how strong or faint the knowledge, only that you find that inner sense of sanction that you deserve what you truly want. If you have trouble finding that inner sanction, try to imagine what it would feel like to know that you deserve what you want. Pretend. It may feel like you are pretending, but your intention is what is important.

4. Make a statement—out loud—about what you desire, but this time describe it as something you deserve.

Examples:

Say: "My heart knows I deserve (*to go to France*)."

Say: "My heart knows I deserve (*an intimate relationship*)."

Say: "My heart knows I deserve (*peace of mind*)."

5. Then if you like, offer gratitude to the Universe for providing you with what you need in its own perfect time.

Example:

Say: "Thank you Universe, for *providing me with whatever I need*."

6. Repeat this sequence for every item on your list or until you use every petal on both flowers.

Delving Deeper

Dialoguing with Your Heart

Your question or statement to your heart is, "My heart knows that I deserve what I desire because ... "

Your Prayer of Intention

After performing the *Rose Petal* Ceremony, describe three steps that you will take this week to remember that you deserve what you desire.

My Heart Knows Affirmations

"My heart knows (*Fill in the blank*)." Repeat five times.

CHAPTER EIGHT

Expressing Your Creative Self

*I merely took the energy it takes to pout
and wrote some blues.*

—Duke Ellington

A fascinating phenomenon took place a number of years ago. A stone statue of the Virgin Mary in a remote church in South America evidently had suddenly begun to weep. The news spread quickly, and people came from all over to see the weeping statue. Scientists came too, of course, and quickly explained what had happened, saying that the humidity in the church had caused moisture to accumulate within the statue's stone over a period of months. Eventually, the stone became saturated with moisture, which condensed and began to seep around the statue's eyes.

To the scientists, the statue's weeping was merely a matter of humidity and condensation and not at all a reflection of something greater taking place, some unknown power at play that can't be seen or explained or understood at all with the mind. But their explanation doesn't account for why the moisture seeped around the statue's eyes, or allow that for this to occur to a statue of the Virgin Mary is incredible to begin with.

Take the Grand Canyon or Handel's *Messiah*. Here too, although there may be a scientific explanation for how the Grand Canyon was formed or how the *Messiah* was composed, the explanation doesn't acknowledge the force or mystery behind their creation. Rational explanation doesn't encompass the miracle of the canyon's formation or the profound, penetrating sound of the "Hallelujah Chorus." It doesn't make room for the inspiration behind creation.

But just because science doesn't deal with inspiration and can't measure it doesn't make inspiration any less real.

Have you ever looked up at a blanket of stars in the sky, watched a spectacular sunset, or witnessed a baby being born? Can you tell me why human beings have the twenty-three pairs of chromosomes they need to develop so perfectly? Why every snowflake is different from all the others? Or why you and I, like snowflakes, each have our own unique form of creative expression?

We do—whether we express it or not. I believe that the different ways in which each of us comes to understand life and expresses our individuality once again reveals the Universe's vast and creative design. *Especially* when we're creating something—whether a casserole, a painting, a knitted sweater, or a human life.

The trouble is that not all of us know how to tap into our creative fire. If this is true for you, look to your musings, to what brings you amusement. Doing so can help bring forth your creative yearnings. That's what the ancient Greeks did, and why they created the myth of the Nine Muses of Creativity.

Believe it or not, the Nine Muses can be *your* muses. They can help you open up to and more deeply appreciate your creative strengths—*and you do have them*. They've been inspiring people throughout history. In ancient times, before poets or storytellers would recite their work, they would often invoke the Muses' inspiration and protection.

According to classical Greek mythology, the Nine Muses were the goddesses who ruled over all of Creativity. In her truly enlightening tape series, *The Second Half of Life*, anthropologist and expert on the Nine Muses, Angeles Arrien, shares that these daughters of Zeus and the goddess Memory represent all the qualities of creativity, including intuition, insight, imagination, life force, and awareness. Messengers between our world and the spirit world, they symbolize all the creativity that we carry in our hearts, from the magical to the worldly to the absurd. Their leader was Apollo, the god of music and harmony, and they lived near the mountains of Helicon and Olympus in Greece. (The Nine Muses are also connected with the liberal arts and sciences. In fact, the word *museum* derives from the Greek word *mouseion*, which means "seat of the muses.")

The first muse is named *Calliope* (pronounced kuh-lie′-ah-pee′). Known as the chief muse, Calliope is the bringer of epic or heroic poetry or stories that have been put to music. Often referred to as "she of the beautiful voice," Calliope holds either a writing tablet or a scroll filled with musical notes.

If you've ever listened to great opera, or if you've ever been mesmerized by the beauty of someone's voice (whether Barbra Streisand's or your daughter's), Calliope has been evoked within you. So what epic poetry are you drawn to, or what poem describes the heroism in your own life? Where does Calliope come alive for you?

Melpomene (pronounced mel-puhm′-eh-nee′) is the muse of tragedy and masks. Angeles Arrien describes

Melpomene as the muse who takes you to your depths, encouraging you to integrate your past hurts and betrayals through reflection and meditation. Known as the "songstress," she's depicted wearing a garland wreath. The garland wreath, symbolizing victory, suggests that you must not hang on to your past wounds and tragedies and become a victim, but rather use them creatively as a way to grow and heal. She asks that you use your disappointment and sorrow to bring your creative passions into the world. She's also shown wearing *cothurnes*, boots traditionally worn by tragic actors.

If you're drawn to the writing of Virginia Woolf or Sylvia Plath, or to the music of the rock group Indigo Girls, you're singing Melpomene's tune. So in what ways have you experienced Melpomene in your life? What masks would it serve you best to remove?

The muse who acknowledges excellence in creativity (particularly writing) and brings it recognition is Clio (pronounced klee'-oh). Known as the "proclaimer," Clio is the muse of writing and history and is often seen sitting with a scroll and accompanied by a chest of books. She is the inspiration behind every book ever written—in particular love stories like *Anna Karenina* and *Romeo and Juliet*. (I suspect she was the inspiration for Alfred Nobel's creating a prize for literature.) Every year, the advertising industry honors their most creative talent with the Clio Awards.

If you're drawn to the works of Jane Austen or Alice Walker, you've called forth Clio into your life. What part of history has captured your attention? The Civil War? The Elizabethan Era? Which historical plays, novels, or love stories have you enjoyed reading? Better yet, where have you written down your own great love story? In your journal? On a yellow pad buried deep in your dresser drawer?

Whatever you've written or have read with heart and soul was inspired by Clio.

Euterpe (pronounced yoo-tur'-pee) is the muse of music or flutes. She is the patron of joy, laughter, and celebration. She has been described as "well pleasing." Euterpe wants you to experience your creativity not as work but as play and love. When you can hardly wait to begin working on a project, she has befriended you. She reminds you that you can bring amusement into your life and into the lives of others and that you can *choose* creative projects that bring you joy.

Remember Mike Meyers's *Austin Powers* and Charlie Chaplin's *Tramp*? They were bursting with the spirit of Euterpe. If Carol Burnett, or Ellen have ever made you split your sides with laughter, Euterpe was laughing right along with you. So what creative acts fill you with glee? Where does your creativity feel like play?

The muse of cosmic poetry, astronomy, and the stars, *Urania* (pronounced yoo-ray'-nee-uh) invites you to use your creativity to understand and express Life's mysteries. Great explorer of the unknown and called "heavenly," Urania reminds you that the Earth, the planets, and the Universe itself are all a fantastic mystery.

So if you're drawn to study the world's deep spiritual explorers, such as the sixteenth-century Hindu poet and ecstatic lover of God, Mirabai, or the thirteenth-century German mystic, Mechtild of Magdeburg, you've been smitten by Urania. If you're a member of the Institute of Noetic Sciences or another organization that studies the mysteries of consciousness and the Universe, or if you belong to a discussion group in your faith community that discusses these issues, Urania is your muse. Known as the "muse of the earth," she carries a golden staff with a silver tip that points to the globe or to the stars, and she foretells the future by the position of the stars. Where has Urania been a part of your life?

Thalia (pronounced thuh-lie'-uh) brings out your laughter and joy through nature, and is called "blooming." The keeper of comedy and nature, Thalia is the queen of parties and festivals that take place in nature. Wearing greenery, flowers, and ivy reeds, and holding a comic mask, Thalia may have lead you to read the story of Moses and other biblical stories about shepherds tending their flocks. She uses her creativity to protect and celebrate the Earth. So if you're a member of Greenpeace or another environmental organization, Thalia lives within you. She spearheads all community events that celebrate the Earth, such as Earth Day and summer and winter solstice celebrations.

If you like to paint nature scenes or photograph nature, if you're a birdwatcher, if you enjoy feeling the cool, fresh air against your skin (whether you're skimming rocks by the seashore or taking a leisurely walk), Thalia is in your soul. If you have a pot of geraniums on your window sill, Thalia is in your heart. She reminds us that the Earth's outer nature mirrors our own inner natures and that being in nature deepens our soul and character.

Terpsichore (pronounced turp-sick'-uh-ree) opens the door to your artistic expression and is the muse of dancing and choral song. Founder and integrator of all the creative and performing arts—song, dance, music, writing, story, drama, healing, and sports—she is present when you're bewitched by all the arts and can't choose among them. Terpsichore believes that no one can live without the arts and has taken it upon herself to ensure that they will survive forever. Remember that last public radio drive you supported? Terpsichore inspired you to contribute, because she's responsible for all the events that help preserve the arts when they are being threatened. If you're a member of your local art museum, she was the muse who inspired you to join.

The most respected of all the muses, Terpsichore surrounds herself with choirs singing or large groups of people dancing. Called "whirler of the dance," she holds a paintbrush in one hand, has a music stand in front of her, and a place to dance in nature beside her. In times of war, hunger, or other hardship, we count on Terpsichore for the inspiration, for example, to send a telegram to a loved one. When times are good, she helps us celebrate variety within the arts. So tell me, where is Terpsichore present in your life? Where is diversity found in your creative expression?

Polymnia (pronounced pah-lim'-nee-uh) is the muse of mime, ceremony, ritual, and geometry. Often shown veiled, she is present at every housewarming and other heartfelt celebrations and rituals you attend—such as circumcisions, baptisms, weddings, and funerals. When you decorate your house for Christmas, Thanksgiving, Chanukah, or Halloween, Polymnia helps you light the candles. She inspires all family traditions, such as handing down to your daughter the ring your mother had handed down to you. If you've ever participated in a sweat lodge, Polymnia was the drummer. Often shown with a pensive look, she wears a crown with little lightning bolts extending from both of her ears. These symbolize our creative awakening.

Remember your last "aha" experience? You have Polymnia to thank for it. The way in which you honor the parts of yourself that you are integrating or releasing is also Polymnia's domain, as is listening to the voice of your heart and inspiring others. Polymnia loves religious dance and theatre, hymns, and pantomime. Because she's the goddess of all sacred poetry, I've called upon her often for inspiration while writing this book (and you may call upon her for inspiration as you work with the Ceremony and Meditation chapters). However, I've also befriended Melpomene, Thalia, Calliope, Euterpe, and Erato.

Erato (pronounced er′-ah-toe′) is the muse of lyric and love poems. Called "lovely," she wears a crown of roses. The sorcerer of the creative fire within, Erato has a burning passion for creativity and believes that whatever creative project you take on must evoke your deepest longing and desire. She believes that the joy and meaning you find in life is connected to this passion. Erato cautions you never to indulge in artistic work that doesn't demand passion and creativity. Rather, she asks, "Where are you seized by a creative project, so much so that you can't stop working on it, there's no time to eat, you must continue on?"

Erato helps us embrace people's similarities and helps us connect with others when we can't speak their language, such as communicating with sign language, laughter, or music. She brings together the different wisdoms of the world, so when the Spirit Rock Buddhist Meditation Center (in northern California) invited the Kripalu Yoga Center (in western Massachusetts) to come and be a part of their curriculum, Erato spearheaded the event. If you attended this seminar or one like it, Erato was your consort.

As you read the descriptions of the Nine Muses, which of them did you resonate with most? You can call on them right now by joining me in performing the *Nine Muses* Ceremony that follows. The *Nine Muses* Ceremony is a fun, enlightening opportunity to honor your creative self. It can help you discover more fully where *your* creative gifts lie and celebrate them in new and meaningful ways. You will invoke the Nine Muses in the same way that you invoked your higher self in Part One.

Whether or not you consider yourself to be creative, I'm sure that as you begin to explore the presence of the Nine Muses in your life, you'll discover that you're more creative than you may have thought. As women, we are all extremely creative—human life emerges from us. The Nine Muses remind us that a life well lived is a work of art.

With that, I invite you to travel with me past Mount Olympus, to the magical, mystical realm of the Nine Muses.

The Nine Muses Ceremony for
Expressing Your Creative Self

There's Euterpe, who brings out your joy and
*   elation,*
Terpsichore, to whom all of art
Is a standing ovation.
Erato ignites you with passion and fire,
Melpomene heals while she's playing her lyre.
Urania shows you the Earth's deepest mystery,
Calliope makes you a lover of history.
And bow down to Clio, who writes all our love
*   stories,*
As Thalia, at sunrise, picks morning glories.
Polymnia is planning the fête of the ages,
Join her—and honor your life's many stages.

In preparation for the *Nine Muses* Ceremony, you will decide which of the muses you would like to invoke as part of the ceremony and the symbol that will represent them. So, begin thinking about which of the Nine Muses have been predominant in your life so far, and which you have not had a relationship with yet, but would like to. To help you ponder, consider the following questions:

- *Where is poetry present in your life? Whose voice(s) do you find mesmerizing?* There you will find Calliope.

- *Where have you enjoyed writing or reading wonderful books or love stories?* There you will find Clio.

- *Where have you used your creativity to help yourself heal and to develop your character?* There you will find Melpomene.

- *Where is your creativity passionately alive in your life?* There you will find Erato.

- *Where are you drawn to creativity in nature?* There you will find Thalia.

- *Where are you drawn to study life's mysteries?* There you will find Urania.

- *Where is your creativity a form of play or where do you use your will to uplift and inspire others with your art?* There you will find Euterpe.

- *Where do you find diversity in your creativity? Do you deeply value the expression of all the arts?* There you will find Terpsichore.

- *When have you had an "aha" experience, been guided by your inner wisdom, or attended a wedding?* There you will find Polymnia.

Use what you've just discovered to help you decide which of these creative nymphs you would like to invoke— which aspects of your creative self you would like to explore.

To help call the muses forth, you will use different symbolic objects that represent each one. Following are some suggested symbols, but feel free to substitute your own. (For further inspiration, call on Polymnia.)

Muses and Their Symbols

- *Clio:* a pen, a book, a writing tablet, your favorite love story (written by you or someone else)

- *Calliope:* a poem, a recording of your favorite singer or opera

- *Melpomene:* a mask, a candle, a vine, a journal with your past hurts written in it, a piece of yarn cut in two

- *Euterpe:* a watch, a representation of an irresistible hobby, a candle, confetti

- *Urania:* a star, a crystal or another representation of the Earth, a spiritual icon (such as the Virgin Mary or the Buddha or a Jewish star), something black

- *Thalia:* a leaf or anything found in nature, a picture of a nature scene, confetti, a heart

- *Terpsichore:* a seed, a paintbrush, music, a pen, other symbols that represent creativity, a colorful object

- *Polymnia:* a light bulb, a candle, a Christmas tree ornament, a menorah, a family heirloom, a wedding band, your symbol for your higher self

- *Erato:* a match, a book that is written in a different language, a creative project

Once you've decided on the muse(s) you will be invoking and their symbols, and have gathered the other materials you will need, which are described next, you're ready to perform the ceremony. Make the ceremony an expression of your creative self. For example, wear something that expresses your creative nature (such as colorful clothing, jewelry, dance slippers, a shawl).

You will need:

- A candle

- Your symbols for the muses—and those aspects of your creative self that you wish to invoke

- A dark object or piece of tarnished silver to represent the dark feminine aspect from which all creativity arises

- A rock to represent your creativity manifesting in the world

- A piece of chocolate to represent the sweetness and joy that comes from creative expression

Directions:

1. Write down on a piece of paper all the ways in which you want to be more creative in your life and the names of the muses you wish to invoke.

2. Think about what may be holding you back from expressing these parts of yourself, and gently release it. (For example, having realistic expectations about your creative projects can help you let go of barriers. Or trusting that you are good enough. You are.)

3. Light the candle.

4. Place the dark object next to the candle.

5. Lift up to your heart the symbol representing the first muse you will be invoking.

6. Say the Nine Muses Invocation (use the invocation following or create your own).

7. Place the muse's symbol next to the dark object alongside the candle.

8. Repeat steps 4–6 for each muse you wish to invoke.

9. Place the rock in front of the candle.

10. After waiting a minute or so, clap your hands loudly several times (in anticipation of achieving your creative goals).

11. Eat the piece of chocolate.

Nine Muses Invocation

Oh Great Goddess of creativity (name of muse), I call upon you to open my heart and help me (state the creative aspect of yourself you wish to express). Live within me as I go about my days. I honor you and that part of myself for which you inspire expression.

Delving Deeper

Dialoguing with Your Heart

Your question or statement to your heart is, "I've learned from having a particular painful experience (thanks to Melpomene) and will express what I have learned creatively by . . . "

Your Prayer of Intention

After performing the *Nine Muses* Ceremony, describe three steps that you will take this week to express your creativity.

Your Heart Knows Affirmations

"My heart knows (*Fill in the blank*)." Repeat five times.

Chapter Nine

Accepting and Honoring
Your Body

I've got a stomach now as well as a behind. And . . .
you can't pull it in both ways . . . [so] I've made it a rule
to pull in my stomach and let my behind look after itself.

—Agatha Christie

*T*he time that I remember using all my energy to wish I was someone else, I was twenty-two years old, riding the subway in Manhattan. A gorgeous, slim woman walked into the subway car. She was thin and angular, with firm little breasts. She didn't need a bra—and she wasn't wearing one.

My eyes immediately became glued to her, as her protruding hipbones, like the tips of opened angel's wings, seemed to whisper in my direction, "Bow down and pray to me, for I am the Thin Goddess. I, alone, can lead you to redemption."

Sucking in my stomach and re-adjusting my bra so that my own breasts wouldn't get out of hand, I stood there and prayed, "God, please let me be *her*."

And that was that. I decided then that, come hell or high water, *I* was going to be thin. But not just thin—*so* thin that people would bow down to me as well. I'd shrink my breasts, flatten my tummy, narrow my hips, and tuck in my thighs.

As an over-achiever, I would find this easy. So, summoning my perfectionist ego self, I set out to complete the task at hand. After a few months of running every day and eating less, I lost the weight I had wanted to lose.

I was thin and I loved it—even buying a bathing suit was enjoyable! I felt like a million bucks. But on a deeper level, I knew that I was really in the poorhouse, because I was seeking the approval of others as a sign of my worthiness. I was running from *myself*.

I had become a slave to the Thin Goddess. What could be a bigger rejection of oneself than rejecting of one's body?

I could cry a thousand years for the heinous crimes I've committed against my body over the years, crimes that so many women have committed. But have you ever thought about why we've been blessed with bodies in the first place? Perhaps, we can come to view our bodies as gifts that provide us with an opportunity to learn about our souls.

After years of looking inward, I've learned that I'm a beautiful, loving, powerful woman exactly as I am—a divine being of God's. I *choose* to accept and nurture my body and the spirit that inhabits it, a choice I must make anew every day.

The ancient Celts have a beautiful metaphor for the human body. They believe that the body is made out of clay and that it comes up out of the earth. So having your feet on the ground connects you to the Earth; you are placing "your private clay on the ancient mother clay from which it has emerged." In his poignant tape series on Celtic wisdom, *Anam Cara,* the scholar and poet John O'Donohue explains that the Celts also believe that because we are made of clay, we come from the underworld or world of Spirit.

For an individual to be in harmony with the world, she must accept her own body as a unique form that has never been found before, one that has a memory and spirit all its own.

Taking the clay metaphor one step further, the life force within each of us brings to our clay what the potter brings to her pot. In other words, we mold and shape the raw clay with which we were born—our bodies—to reflect our inner selves and our life's journey. Just as each clay form the potter creates has its own unique potential (such as to hold flowers or food), our bodies, too, have a unique, divine potential.

Me, I've discovered that I'm a soup tureen, filled with goodness and wholeness, made from clay that was found where the Earth's greatest treasures have been excavated— the kind of soup tureen you'd be proud to place on your table. Once I *finally* accepted myself as a soup tureen, I discovered that people love my soup. That's when I started serving others what was truly mine—and nourishing myself as well.

It is through our bodies that we can come to know our souls. Have you ever caught a glimpse of your soul? Have you ever had the experience where your body "drops away" and you experience yourself (and possibly someone else) as pure spirit? Perhaps you have had this kind of experience when you were making love with someone or at another equally intimate time.

There are certain times when our bodies are more alive than ever. If you've ever practiced yoga, you may have experienced how your body's wisdom leads you through a posture flow. Or if you've ever had a massage, you may have noticed how your body lets you know exactly what it needs.

Even if you've never practiced yoga or had a massage,

you can become more aware of and in tune with your body. For example, you can pay attention to your body's urgings for more sleep, nourishment, or relaxation. You can attend to the bodily cues you may receive when your heart knows something of importance. You can heed the inner urge that moves you toward realizing your divine potential.

In order to become aware of your body's wisdom, you may have some healing to do. We all do. So take a minute now and think back on the ways in which you may have abandoned your body over the years. Have there been parts of your body that you've abused or neglected, of which you must now ask forgiveness?

If there are, you're in good company. In fact, I asked a group of women that very question and received some telling responses. Marsha asked her face for forgiveness. She had hated her face because it revealed her disappointment and sadness, even when she tried to hide it. Mary Jean apologized to her breasts for disliking them because they were too big, and Cindy to her hips and thighs for the same reason.

Esther asked her arms for forgiveness, for not bringing them out into the light of day—she hadn't worn sleeveless dresses in years because she was embarrassed by the way her skin hung down. "It's time," she said, "to take my arms out of the closet." I'm sure that had I asked this question of more women, it wouldn't have been long before, collectively, we would have been asking forgiveness from every inch of our beautiful bodies.

Self-forgiveness isn't easy to allow. The loathing that we carry around for our bodies may be more than skin deep. It may have been passed down to us from our mothers, grandmothers, and great grandmothers, forged into the very memories of our cells, and it is reinforced every time we pick up a women's magazine or go shopping for clothes.

Indeed, the negative body image that women suffer from has deep cultural roots. Even the story of Adam and Eve reflects the assumption that, since Eve was born from Adam's rib, she was of less worth than he was. Rising above these oppressive attitudes takes a daily commitment not to give in to those inner voices that tell us that we have to hold it in here, or tuck or hide it away there, or avoid letting our bodies become like those of our mothers.

No more! Why not spend some time discovering the beauty and mystery of *your* body with the *Loving Body* Ceremony that follows. The *Loving Body* Ceremony can help you love and respect your body exactly as it is. It can help you see that you are a beautiful, unique soul who inhabits a glorious human temple. It can guide you to find compassion for that vulnerable, delicate, yet strong woman inside, who may be blinded to her true magnificence.

Whatever your body issues (whether you think you're too fat, too thin, too plain, too wrinkled, too hairy, too anything), performing the ceremony can help you let it all go. It invites you to observe your body, without judgment, from a detached yet loving state, so that you can release those judgments and replace them with acceptance and love.

This may be may be an especially tender experience for you. So have self-compassion. If feeling kindness toward your body seems impossible, then pretend. Imagine what it would feel like if you did have compassion and respect for your body. Only by accepting your body exactly as it is can you make any changes you may want to make in a responsible, healthy way.

Won't you join me in discovering the sacredness of your own loving body? If not now, when?

The Loving Body Ceremony for Accepting and Embracing Your Body

I am not my body. I am the divine spirit who inhabits it.
I love and honor my body exactly as it is.
As I listen to the cues my body gives me, I am wisely led.
I carry my body with grace and ease, loving the way it moves.
I forgive myself for abusing my body, and will care for it with loving compassion.

In preparation for the *Loving Body* Ceremony, make an intention to be open to the experience. Acknowledge yourself for your self-love and bravery. The ceremony calls for you to stand naked in front of a full-length mirror, then to gently and lovingly acknowledge and bless the different parts of your body. This process may feel a bit intimidating at first, especially if you usually avoid looking at yourself naked. But remember, the more uncomfortable you are, the greater the opportunity to become free of your judgments and inhabit your own skin. (If you absolutely can't perform the ceremony naked, then perform it wearing your bra and panties.) Once you have the items you will need listed next, you'll be ready to perform the ceremony.

You will need:

- A full-length mirror

- An outfit you love to wear, one that honors your body

- A chair, if needed

Directions:

1. Read aloud the *Loving Body Affirmation*, slowly and clearly, following the instructions; or record it beforehand—very slowly, pausing as often as you like—and play it back as you perform the ceremony; or you can download the ceremony from my website at www.your heartknows.com.

2. When you complete the ceremony, sit quietly for a few minutes to integrate your experience.

3. Dress in the special outfit you've selected.

Loving Body Affirmation

Remove your clothes and step in front of the mirror.
Feel your feet on the floor.
Feel your body as it breathes in and out.
Now think of your body as a vessel of your essence—
   the spirit who inhabits it.
Feel your body as the sacred home of your spirit.
This experience is for your body and your spirit.
It is a journey that will take you "outside" your body
   for a short while,

So that you can view it from a new perspective,
From a more detached state,
Where you are less bound by judgment.
You'll observe your body from head to toe,
Taking it all in with new eyes.
You will really see your body—as if for the first time.
You will really feel your body.
Then, after you've finished,
You'll "step back into" your body
Returning home, again, with a new and more loving
       perspective.
Now, close your eyes,
Allow your spirit to gently step outside your body
A few inches to the left of it.
Leave your body right there for just a moment
And breathe.
In a few minutes, you'll open your eyes,
And you will see your body from slightly afar
From a more detached and open state.

Now, open your eyes
And look at your body.
See your body with a new, detached perspective.
See the physical casing that encloses the spirit who is
       looking back at it
From a slight distance.
Your spirit is the witness.
Your spirit sees that your body is not who YOU are,
YOU are the essence who is watching.
Now, take in your body with your eyes,
Slowly looking at it from head to toe.
Witness your body at this moment in your life,
Dropping all judgment.

And see what your physical home looks like.
There is no judgment in the center of your soul.
There is only what is.
Now, see your body through the eyes of loving
  compassion.
Honor this body,
That has kept you safe and warm
Since the day you were born.
This body which has given you shelter as you've made
  your way on Earth
And carried out your deeds.
Your body is here to be loved,
For you could not exist in the world without it.
Your body is a sacred temple.
A shrine.
Your holy dwelling place.
Love your body, for it is the body that you have.
It is a manifestation of all your experiences and
  expectations.
It has served you well.
Know that your body is not stagnant.
It is ever changing . . .
Always reflecting who you are in the moment.
If you find yourself judging your body, simply let the
  judgment go
Now, celebrate this body you inhabit.
  Celebrate your feet.
Feel them standing solidly on the ground below.
Notice your toes, the balls of your feet, your heels.
Touch them, move them, massage them—
Thanking your feet for grounding you in your life
And taking you wherever you go.
Now slowly move up and

Celebrate your legs.
Notice their shape and the texture of their skin.
Place your hands on your ankles and
Slowly work your way up to your calves and past your
knees.
Feel your legs from top to bottom.
Love them, also, for getting you to and fro—
day in and day out.
Now move your hands up and
Celebrate your thighs.
Sensual, vulnerable, waiting to be caressed.
Love the soft suppleness of your thighs.
Now move your hands behind and
Celebrate your buttocks.
Honor them for their delicious roundness
And the pleasure they bring you when they're softly
caressed.
Gently stroke your buttocks, thanking them
For always giving you such a cozy cushion to sit down
upon.
Now return to your front, up past your pelvis and
Celebrate your belly.
Honor its softness, hardness, roundness, flatness
Its essence of your femaleness.
Your belly knows.
Deep down, it knows
Where you must go and
What you must do to recognize your wholeness
It knows when you are safe,
And when you are in danger.
It is the core of your being
Pregnant with love, creativity, and joy.
Now move your hands up and

Celebrate your breasts.
Feel your breasts exactly as they are,
The milk of your compassion—
Your breasts, which may have nourished children,
Or may sometime in the future.
Soft, supple, sensual, loving, open, strong.
Thank your breasts, those visions of loveliness
For remaining ever so close to your heart.
Celebrate your heart.
Know that your open heart is the doorway to every-
thing you desire.
It is where you cherish the things which you value
most.
Breathe, opening your heart to the day.
Now move your hands out and
Celebrate your arms.
They help you reach what you need,
To create the life you want.
Notice their contour and shape, their muscle and flesh.
Feel your arms.
Now move your hands up and
Celebrate your shoulders.
Gently feel their bones, muscle, and skin,
And give them thanks for all their support.
Now, slowly move your hands past your neck to your
face.
Be delicate as you embrace
This place where you become intimate with the world.
Celebrate your mouth.
See how your lips shape the words you speak,
The kisses you bestow.
Notice their color, shape, wetness, dryness.
Now, move up and

Celebrate your nose.
Your nose, which carries your breath,
And gives you life.
Notice its contour, its shape.
It is the one nose you have to
Gently take in a breath and then let it go.
Now, move up and
    Celebrate your eyes.
Appreciate their color, softness, and intensity.
It is through those very eyes that
Your physical world exists—the beauty and the pain.
Now, move up and
    Celebrate your hair.
Lovely filaments.
Run your hands through your hair.
Feel its texture.
See its color.
Notice how your hair frames your face
And makes you look so uniquely "you."
Look at your entire face for a few moments.
Take in its exquisite style.

Now, place your hands back down at your sides,
And with your eyes, celebrate your glorious physique.
Take in your unique magnificence.
Embrace all the parts of your divine bodily creation.
The shape of your ankles.
The curve of your calves.
The suppleness of your thighs.
The possibility of your belly.
The divinity of your breasts.
The contour of your neck.
The shape of your nose.

The wisdom in your eyes.
The texture of your hair.
The "feel" of your skin.
Take in all that you physically are
In this glorious moment.
God's and your mutual creation.
And know that who you are is ever changing.
Your skin always breathing.
Your cells dying and regenerating.
And know that even though you can change
The appearance of your body,
Your true beauty always remains within.

Now, close your eyes and allow your spirit
To gently step back into your body.
And behold yourself in the mirror, once again.
Take in the divinity of your most sacred human
    temple.

🎵 Delving Deeper

Dialoguing with Your Heart

Your question or statement to your heart is, "Loving my body is important to me because . . . "

Your Prayer of Intention

After performing the *Loving Body* Ceremony, describe three steps that you will take this week to accept and honor your body.

My Heart Knows Affirmations

"My heart knows (*Fill in the blank*)." Repeat five times.

CHAPTER TEN

Opening to a Spiritual Partnership

*If we can find the whole world in a grain of sand, we can
also find the soul itself at the small point in life
where destinies cross and hearts intermingle.*

—Thomas Moore

$\mathcal{S}$omeone whom I love dearly told me recently that her husband was leaving her after ten years of marriage. I was stunned. I thought about her two children, aged six and eight, who hadn't yet heard the news. How their bright, sunny faces would probably soon darken with anguish, dread, and fear. I cried for them, and I cried for me, remembering how devastated I was when my parents got divorced.

But even before her husband left her, my friend never seemed content. She's the type of person who is kind to a fault—always caring about other people more than about herself. I sensed somehow that her caring was due, in part, to a lack of self-worth. Somewhere inside, she believed that other people's needs were more important than hers. Her husband had serious health problems, and he had demanded a lot from her. She had always put his needs first. Now he was gone.

One day while we were talking on the phone, I suggested that she might look at this crisis in her life as an opportunity to learn how to truly take care of *herself*. When a woman does not live as her higher self in the context of an intimate relationship, I posed, the relationship can't foster self-growth and, therefore, can't be truly satisfying. Unless your relationship nurtures depth and intimacy, you cannot continue to grow within the content of the relationship. It doesn't matter how many relationship workshops you've taken.

My friend is not alone. Unfortunately, many of us have been in relationships in which we lacked self-esteem, in which our hearts were telling us, "Leave, he doesn't treat you right"—but we didn't trust ourselves enough to listen. Ultimately, we may need to learn that it's better to be alone than to be in a relationship in which we're not truly known or loved. When we give up our self-respect to be with someone else, we lose ourselves.

Your higher self wouldn't choose to be in a relationship that doesn't foster growth. She'd choose a soulful, spiritual partnership. A spiritual partnership is one in which two people are committed to using their relationship as a vehicle for growth. Their romance is a rocket ship that propels them to experience their full potential for self-awareness. They understand that they were brought together for healing purposes, not to hide from their weaknesses, but to move past them. They're ready to turn their hurts into sacred wounds by making their relationship a sacred entity. They've come together to learn the true meaning of love.

The minister at my husband's and my wedding, also a dear friend and kindred spirit, told our guests during the ceremony that a spiritual partnership is the toughest teacher that two people can have. People burst out laughing—the way you laugh when you know you've heard the truth.

In a spiritual partnership, your partner will bear witness to the places inside of you that need healing, and reflect these places back to you with lights that could illuminate Carnegie Hall. Because you're free to fully be yourself, all your inner demons and those of your partner will come to light. Anytime there's a chance for love so deep, there is a wall of fire that you must go through. Baby, you're going to burn.

If you really want to become an expert at distinguishing the voice of your heart from the voices in your head, be in a spiritual partnership. Since the focus of your relationship is on deepening self-knowledge, you'll have thousands of opportunities to recognize when you aren't coming from the heart. Even if you're someone like me, who used to always want things to be "nice" and who didn't like to feel or express her anger, sooner or later the person you love will touch a wound inside of you that will send your heart reeling. And those voices in your head will be saying things that will make you question whether you have a heart at all.

When my husband Bill used to become very busy with work and other personal commitments, he would sometimes withdraw from me emotionally. Although I knew the withdrawal wasn't intentional, I still found it painful. One time when this happened, I became enraged. After a day and a half of pouting and being miserable, I knew that even though it would be the hardest thing to do, I would have to acknowledge my upset before I could let it go.

So, I decided to tell Bill how angry I was, how the anger was holding me back, and what I needed from him. Because I no longer blamed him, he was able to hear me, and I felt acknowledged, as did he. From this experience,

I learned more deeply that love is not about getting something from someone else or about changing them. *Everything* that had transpired between us—all the arguing and the making up—*was us loving each other*. In the context of a spiritual partnership, whether making love or fighting, it's all the same thing: living, learning, and loving.

Have you had a similar experience? Whether you're in a relationship now or have been in one in the past, have the voices in your head sent you to places that your heart didn't want to go? And, when you worked out whatever you needed to with your partner or within yourself, did you feel stronger, knowing more fully who you were, who your partner was, and what new gifts the relationship had to offer?

Right now, bring yourself into stillness. Dwell on the following questions and see what arises: If you're *not* in a relationship right now, are you looking for one? Or do you need to spend some time alone, and why? Do you like yourself? Are you having fun? Are you *afraid* of being in a true spiritual partnership? Do you crave having one more than anything in the world?

If you're *in* a relationship, does it continually take you deeper within yourself and challenge you to renew yourself? Is it a sacred dance between you and your eternally beloved? How are you doing in the romance department? Have you ever experienced a time when the two of you were so enveloped in each other's body, mind, and spirit that you no longer knew where you ended and they began? Or is your relationship lacking this kind of intimacy, and is it a kind you'd like to experience?

Are you in the right relationship altogether? Not all spiritual partnerships are meant to last forever—only as long as the living, learning, and loving continues. If your relationship isn't working, can you get it back on track? Or should you leave and be alone for a while, so that you can make space, physically, emotionally, and soulfully for the perfect partner to come along at the perfect time?

It seems that most of the lessons we must learn throughout our lives relate to the self—self-compassion, self-will, self-worth, self-forgiveness, self-reliance, self-knowledge, self-respect. Not surprisingly, we must often do this inner work outside the context of a relationship. Only then can we open ourselves to experiencing true love with a partner. We may have to be alone to heal from relationships that have wounded our hearts and damaged our self-esteem. We may have to forgive someone for treating us badly. Or we may have to forgive ourselves for allowing the ill treatment. Only after we do this inner work is a spiritual partner able to reflect back to us who we truly are.

As women who are following the wisdom of our hearts, it is our desire—our calling—to evoke from our intimate relationships that which we long for most. Perhaps that's to be seen and loved for who we are, as we fulfill our divine potential in life. And more than that, this kind of love is an expression of divine love, being one with everyone and everything.

When you find your beloved, honor the sacred mystery that brought the two of you together. From the day you meet until the day you part, never belittle or tamper with the mysterious power that enabled your hearts to recognize one another. Only when you acknowledge love's mystery can you experience its rapture.

Unfortunately, after a while it's easy to lose your awareness of love's divine play by psychoanalyzing your relationship or trying to change your partner's personality—when it was truly his or her heart that called you into partnership in the first place. Life's ups and downs have a way of anesthetizing us to the miracle that brought us and our partner together. We can lose sight of the divine gift the relationship truly is.

When your life is so closely entwined with another person's, you run the risk of losing your sense of self and beginning to depend on the other person for your own happiness. Or you can remain *too* independent, afraid to surrender yourself to love, thereby sacrificing a deeper intimacy that you may truly crave. Our ego self always wants to be right. And, in an intimate relationship, it has endless opportunities to make our partner wrong.

It takes work to keep the spark of romance alive. Without doing the work, the mystery—the romance—can die. Just as you must add wood to a fire, or it will smolder, so too must you tend to the flame of your romance. This tending calls for a commitment to nurture that which the two of you share. It takes forgiveness, compassion, and the ability to honor your partner's purity of heart. It takes being together in the not-knowing, leaving your presumptions behind. It calls for revering the mystery that brought you and your partner together and allowing the mystery to unravel.

In the Celtic tradition, "soul partners" are two people whose essences lay together in the clay of the Earth before they were born. Once their two souls take separate bodies in the physical world, they roam the ends of the Earth longing for one another until they find each other again. True love is born from this mysterious, romantic seed.

In the Jewish tradition, a single soul divides into the male and the female before coming to Earth. Each half then goes in search of the other. Jews hope that, when two people marry, the marriage indeed celebrates the two halves of one soul coming together.

Now, in the spirit of love, I invite you to join me in celebrating, honoring, and reaffirming the love for your spiritual partner (whether or not you are already with this person) by performing the *Mystical Romance* Meditation that follows. If you're *in* a relationship, the meditation can help you tend to the sacred fire that will keep your romantic flame burning. It can allow you to become quiet inside, so that you can more deeply connect with the love you share and allow it to grow.

If you are *not* in a relationship, the meditation can help open your heart and draw your spiritual partner near. In stillness, you may find the path that leads your sacred lover to your door. Whatever your romantic experiences have been like in the past, you can embrace love's mystery more fully. It's time to have the romantic relationship that you've always dreamed about, the one that, in the past, you may have shied away from, the one your heart knows belongs to you.

The Mystical Romance Meditation for Opening to a Spiritual Partnership

My sacred lover is on the way to me.
I see my partner's innocence, I feel my partner's love.
Although we I have merged as one, I will never forget who I am as an individual.
I am vulnerable with my lover. I am myself.
I will never take my lover for granted.

During the *Mystical Romance* Meditation you will be led through a basic body-scan and then be guided to open your heart to a spiritual partner, who may or may not exist in your life right now. (See the section on Techniques for Guided Meditation in Chapter Five for tips on conducting the meditation.)

Directions:

Sit or lie in a comfortable position. Close your eyes and begin to take slow deep breaths, feeling the air going in through your nose and down your throat to your chest, and up and out through your nose again. Allow yourself to become calmer and the muscles throughout your body to relax. Let any tension from the day dissolve. Allow the weight of your body to sink into the floor or chair, feeling how your body is supported by it and by the earth below. Now let your breathing return to normal, while paying attention to your breath as it goes in and out. Do this for a few minutes.

In your mind's eye, imagine yourself walking down a road. It can be a country road, a trail in the woods, whatever kind of road comes into your mind. See yourself walking down the road and taking in your surroundings. Perhaps you notice some tall evergreen trees, birds, or rocks. Perhaps you notice a big field in the distance. See what you notice. (Pause)

You continue walking. When you find a place that looks comfortable and safe, look around to make sure that you are alone—and stop. After looking around once more, to make sure that you are alone, slowly remove the armor shield that you're wearing around your torso, like a tight sweater—the shield that protects your heart—and gently place it on the ground. Immediately you feel lighter, freer.

Begin thinking about your special, sacred lover (or imagined lover). Begin to feel your love for that person well up in your heart. If you have a partner, perhaps you can see your partner's face and feel your partner's presence in your body. If your partner is unknown to you, enjoy the anticipation of a special love that's yet to come. Imagine yourself sending your love out to this special person, your soul partner, knowing that the love you're sending will bring this partner to you. And wait.

A few moments later, you see someone coming toward you. You know it is the soul partner whom your love has carried to you. Your partner reaches you, and you both stand face to face. You touch each other's bodies, gently. You acknowledge to yourself how your partner supports you in everything you do, and your partner acknowledges you.

Then the love you're feeling for your partner wells up inside of you so strongly that it rises up out of you in the form of your soul. Your lover experiences the same thing. Your two souls or essences, which look like energy or light or whatever you imagine souls to look like, are floating next to each other above your heads. Imagine what they look like. (Pause)

Your essences are ancient partners that have danced together in eternity. Each holds a sacred responsibility for the other—holding each other's dreams and nurturing each other's souls. Both of you know that even when you're apart, the special bond you share will always keep you together.

Your eyes meet with a look of sacred recognition. You smile and give your partner a special gift. See the gift in your mind's eye, let it emerge from your imagination. (Pause)

Your partner receives your gift and gives you one in return. Then you both smile, and your partner kisses you softly on the lips. Your partner says, "I must leave," promising that you will be together again when the sun goes down. You nod and watch your lover walk away, knowing that your love for each other is a sacred gift that will last forever in your hearts. Leaving your armor shield where it is on the ground, you begin walking down the same road from which you came, and into the rest of your day.

When you are ready to end the ceremony, begin, once again, to notice your breath going in and out, as you become aware of your body sitting in your chair or lying on the floor. Begin to wiggle your toes and fingers. Then open your eyes. Notice if you feel warmth emanating from your heart or surrounding your entire body. See if you are more open to feeling the love that you have for your partner. If there is an issue between your partner and yourself, has it become less painful? If you don't have a partner right now, notice if you are more open to having one.

Delving Deeper

Dialoguing with Your Heart

Your question or statement to your heart is: "The love I have attracted in my life . . . "

Your Prayer of Intention

After performing the *Mystical Romance* Meditation, describe three steps that you will take this week to keep your romance alive or to draw your spiritual partner near.

My Heart Knows Affirmations

"My heart knows (*Fill in the blank*)." Repeat five times.

CHAPTER ELEVEN

Discovering Your Truth
in the Moment

And Yes I said yes I will yes.

— Molly Bloom, in James Joyce's *Ulysses*

*H*ave you ever thought about the fact that years from now *you'll* be to future generations what your ancestors are to you? Dead as a doornail. Have you ever stopped for a minute in the midst of your busy afternoon and realized that, someday, you'll probably be somebody's great-, great-, great-, great-grandmother, aunt, or cousin—a fleeting thought at best—even if your legacy lives on in people's hearts for centuries?

I have, not long ago, while driving through the neighborhood I grew up in. My mother, pointing out the car window, had just told me that only seventy-five years earlier, our typical New York City neighborhood had cows roaming up and down its dirt roads.

Well, the thought of Bessie the cow grazing leisurely next to P.S. 96 in the Bronx got me thinking about life's changes. I realized that the world is changing *fast*, and whatever it's going to be like in three hundred years from now, *I* will not be around to experience it. Just as you and I learned about the ancient Greeks and Romans in high school, the people of the future will eat their food, play their games, and live out their lives without ever knowing that *we* existed at all.

Now, I realize that this point seems rather obvious. But where does the truth of it leave us? Does it make *our* lives any less significant?

No.

This impermanence can actually highlight the significance of our lives, when we become aware that *these are the very lives we've been given.* It's up to *us* to choose how to live them.

So why do we spend so much of the time lost in the future or worrying about the past, instead of living in the present moment? The minute we become present, its benefits—such as calmness and clarity—are so obvious, it's a throwaway. Yet, that's exactly what so many of us do with the present moment—we throw it away. "Wish you were here" is what the present moment would say to the majority of us, most of the time.

But perhaps there are times that you'd *rather* focus on the future or ruminate about the past than be in the present moment. Perhaps the present moment hasn't dealt you a hand you'd care to play. Perhaps you're wondering, "What's all the fuss about living in the present moment, anyway?" Living in the present moment can be difficult, especially when we're confused or are in pain.

Still, when you live in the present moment, you're *in* the game of life—you're up at bat, not sitting on the sidelines. True, you can strike out. You can fail miserably, be embarrassed, humiliated, make a complete fool of yourself. But standing at the plate, with that silly bat in your hand, is the *only* way you can live as an empowered person, experience self-love, or truly connect with others and with God.

The present moment is where your thirst for life bubbles over. It's where your creative sparks ignite. She who illuminates all things to you—your higher self—can only communicate with you in the Now. So if you want a good reality check—get present!

For example, when your baby is screaming for her bottle, the present moment will *make sure* you know—whether you're tired or busy or all out of bottles or formula. When you're hungry, you'll know—as soon as you become present to your growling stomach—and you'll usually know exactly what you're hungry for. However, if you're not physically hungry yet crave food, the chances are that you're not in the present moment at all. Rather, you may be caught up in the past—ruminating about an old hurt, for example—and are using food to comfort yourself, numb your pain, or punish yourself. (The same holds true for cravings for alcohol, drugs, or other substances.)

So, like me, you may sometimes find yourself avoiding the present moment because it's painful. When this happens, close your eyes and breathe. Breathing will bring you right back into the moment and to what you're feeling. Then you'll know exactly what to do, even if that's NOTH-ING—even if that means not taking any action until you gain more clarity. I've learned that becoming present is the first step toward breaking old patterns and making choices that are more aligned with my truth. Wherever I find myself in the present moment, it's exactly where I need to be. From there, the right actions always arise.

Think about the people in your life who are peaceful, content, who look healthy, and who are living empowered lives. Then think about the people who aren't. You'll find that those who have a greater sense of health and well-being are living in the present moment, and that those who don't, aren't. Likewise, when *you're* feeling powerful, clear, and strong in your intentions, you're present to Life.

You *present* or offer yourself to Life. You have a *presence* or a sense about you that rubs off on people and draws them to you. You're more aware of your senses, including your sixth sense, the voice of your heart. So, another powerful way to bring yourself back into the moment is simply to become aware of your body and your senses. Pay attention to what you're seeing, hearing, or touching, or do a brief body-scan.

"But what if I don't like my body?" you may be wondering.

If you don't like your body, then the *last* thing you'd want to do is become present to it, right?

Wrong.

Trying to avoid being uncomfortable is one of the biggest injustices we can inflict upon ourselves. Yet, we've learned that life is always supposed to be comfy cozy, that we're never supposed to feel any sorrow, uneasiness, or pain. We've been taught that feeling pain is "bad," that we should avoid feeling it at all costs. If this is how you live your life, then you're probably not living in the present moment very much at all.

And you're paying the price.

You're not fully living. You're half-dead, unable to truly smell the flowers, experience love, have fun, be spontaneous, create the life you want.

As much as you may try, you can never *really* avoid the present moment anyway. Reality always has a way of sneaking up on you, if it hasn't already knocked you over the head. Keep in mind that, to the extent that you shut out pain, you also shut out joy. That's the way it works. So, it's really up to you. If you want to experience life's riches and joys in their divine abundance, you have to be present for *everything* that life has to offer. In other words, you must *choose* whatever life brings your way.

"Choose to have my car break down? Choose to have my husband leave me? Choose to have someone whom I love pass away?" you may be asking.

In a certain sense, yes. I'm not saying that you should *want* something painful to happen to you. I'm saying that if it does happen and you choose to accept it, you won't be resisting life. And resisting life is what causes you to suffer. I'm not saying that you should want to have someone you love die. I'm saying that choosing to accept his or her passing in your own time and way, rather than harboring anger or bitterness, will help you heal your pain and, in time, find contentment once again.

Saying yes to the present moment is saying yes to Life. It's honoring Life with your truth, whether that truth includes an awareness of anger, disappointment, doubt, fear, jealousy, joy, compassion, ecstasy, or divine love. All we ever *really* have is the present moment—that fertile, abundant place that holds our deepest longings, our pain and our joy, the place that waits for us all.

When was the last time that you blessed Life with your presence and blessed yourself by being present to Life? This minute? An hour ago? Last month? Last year? There are so many ways that you can bring yourself into the Now. These include doing yoga or meditation, taking a walk in nature, jogging or exercising, or becoming absorbed in whatever you're doing. All you need is the *desire* to be present, and you're three-quarters of the way there.

Fortunately, an opportunity to open up to the Now awaits you with the *Fields of Now* Meditation that follows. The *Fields of Now* Meditation will help bring you into the present moment, so that you see reality with new eyes—with a spark of clarity. During the experience, you will receive a special message from the core of your being or heart—your truth in the moment—that can guide you in your life.

What do you say? Whether you're ready to feel the truth sparks fly, or simply want to relax into the moment, how about joining me in the magical, mystical realm of Now . . .

The Fields of Now Meditation for Discovering Your Truth in the Moment

Come frolic in the fields of Now,
Where life bubbles over
And truth sparks fly—
Where the beat of your heart
Reflects the light in your eyes.
Where pain is real, but you move through it—
Get past it.
Where each new moment is a perfect surprise.
Come frolic the fields of Now.
And Yes I am yes I am yes.

During the *Fields of Now* Meditation you will be led through a basic body-scan and then be guided to find the life force or "spark of Now" that's present within. The spark will reveal your special message from your core, your heart—your truth in the moment.

Directions:

Lie down in a comfortable position. Make sure that your body is relaxed. Close your eyes and begin to take slow, deep breaths, becoming aware of your body as you're inhaling and exhaling. Feel the weight of your body sink into the floor or bed as it supports you, as you continue breathing in and out for a few minutes. (Pause)

Notice if you feel any sensations throughout your body, or in a particular area of your body, such as a tingling or throbbing or sensation. If you do, allow it to exist—don't force or try to change anything. Just notice.

Now gently turn your attention to your feet. Notice if you feel tension in the bottoms of your feet or in your toes or ankles, as you breathe softly into these body parts, allowing them to relax. Now move your attention up to your shins, calves, and knees. Wiggle your legs slightly, allowing any tension in these areas to softly release, as you breathe into these areas. Now while remaining aware of your breathing, move your attention up to your thighs and pelvic area, sending them the healing energy of your breath. Repeat this process of focusing, breathing, and relaxing, moving up through your belly, torso, chest, arms, neck, face, and crown of your head.

When you've finished, once again become aware of your entire body. Notice what it feels like. Is it more relaxed than when you began this meditation? Less relaxed? The same? See if you feel any sensations throughout your body. Be present. Breathe into the Now.

Now allow your breath to connect you with the core of your being—the still place within. Feel your breath, your life force, fill your core until you can no longer distinguish between the two—until your breath and your core essence have become one. (Pause)

In your mind's eye, notice what your core energy feels like. Perhaps it feels sparkly or sweet, fiery or wispy. Perhaps it's so subtle you can hardly feel it at all. Notice what it looks like. Perhaps it looks like a ball of fire pulsating in and out, revealing your determination to have what you want in your life. Perhaps it radiates a quiet stillness, reflecting your inner stillness. Perhaps it reveals your connection to all living things—the sky, the birds, your next-door neighbor, people living in far-away countries, the plants and animals that cover the Earth. See and feel the energy that connects you to the Now, to yourself, to everything that exists. (Pause)

This energy, when it's ignited, is a spark that can reveal your truth to you. Right now. In this very moment. Not tomorrow. Not yesterday. Now. Breathe into the spark or energy and discover the special message that's there waiting for you—your truth in the Now. If you have a decision you've been pondering or if you want some guidance, ask now, and be open to your message. Have no expectations about what the message should be or the way in which it should be revealed to you. Welcome it in whichever form it comes, whether in words ... or sensations ... or a different kind of knowing. (Pause)

After you receive your message, acknowledge your core essence with a gentle nod from within. Thank your core for sharing this valuable message with you, even if the message doesn't seem important or doesn't make any sense. You don't have to understand or like the message that you received. Trust that the wisdom of it will make sense to you when it's supposed to.

Now, gently let the spark begin to fade away, as you connect, once again, with your breath. Thank the Now for illuminating your special message to you.

 Delving Deeper

Dialoguing with Your Heart

Your question or statement to your heart is, "The message I received during the meditation . . . "

Your Prayer of Intention

After performing the *Fields of Now* Meditation, describe three steps that you will take this week to live in the present moment.

My Heart Knows Affirmations

"My heart knows (*Fill in the blank*)." Repeat five times.

Afterword

The other day I was sitting on the beach with my sixteen-month-old son, Lucas. He was in his stroller and I was crouched down beside him. It was his first time on the beach, and I was pointing out to him the ocean, sand, and sky. He took it all in the way that sixteen-month-olds do, and as I watched his face light up with joy I, too, saw the beach as if for the first time. It was one of the sweetest moments of my life.

Suddenly, I realized that *this* was the moment my heart had kept on telling me I would experience, but all those years I struggled to create our family, I didn't believe.

In hindsight, I could say, "I wish I knew then what I know now . . . ," but it wouldn't be true. I did know, I just didn't trust. I could say, "I wish I had trusted . . . " But then, perhaps, the moment wouldn't have been as sweet.

Working with Your Journal Components as *Sacred Pages*

Filling your *sacred pages* is a simple process and can be deeply gratifying, especially if you hold an attitude of wonder and awe when working with the components. Again, think of working with them as delving deeper to discover who you *really* are, which is not only your privilege, but also your birthright. To open yourself to your journaling experience, to make it as powerful and as meaningful as it can be, you would do well to remember the following:

Hold a Sacred Attitude

Let the pen you are using to fill your *sacred pages* symbolize the sanctity of the messages you receive from your heart. You may want to use a special pen saved just for this purpose.

When you write, allow the act of writing to become like a yoga practice—the practice of flowing with what you know and feel inside. Know that as the ink touches the paper, the *truth* of what you write will be forever etched on the page and in your soul.

Read Over What You've Written

If you're anything like me, you may sometimes be tempted to gloss over your words quickly, especially in the *Dialoguing with Your Heart* sections. Instead, open your heart and mind to the messages you receive, so that you can integrate what you've written and make the words your own.

You may find that what you read doesn't seem like the truth. If this happens, put your journal away for a day or so. Then go back and re-read the pages. The chances are that the distance will give you a new perspective and clarity from which to view your experience. (When I read over my *sacred pages* after a day or two, I usually think, "Of course. Why did I ever doubt that?") *Never doubt what you've written.* You'll see that the deeper the level from which the messages come, the more they reflect your inner awareness.

When you've finished working with any of the components, spend a few moments in silence. Do you feel complete? Is there more for you to explore? You may get a message even after you've finished writing. That's fine. Write it down then.

Trust Yourself and the Process

Don't be concerned if you don't feel that you received as full an experience as you would have liked, or if you didn't remain peaceful or non-resistant. The biggest obstacles you can come across when working through the process are judgment and fear. If you experience any judgment or fear, simply acknowledge it and let it go. Rest assured that your heart and mind were open whether or not you knew it, sensed it, or believed it. In fact, your heart has known all along what your mind may have just discovered.

Dialoguing with Your Heart

- When you're ready to begin, read the assigned question or statement and begin responding with the first thought that comes into your mind. (If you want, you can answer your own question, instead of, or in addition to, the question given.) Just write down what comes into your mind, even if it feels as though you're making it up.

- Allow the information to come very quickly as the internal messages go back and forth between you and your heart. Don't worry about grammar or spelling. Just keep your pen moving.

- If you find yourself judging the messages you receive, notice that you're judging and write down what you hear anyway. (Although I still judge myself sometimes, I no longer let it stop me.)

- Open up to the flow. The fuel for really taking off with this powerful process is having an open heart and mind.

Example:

Following is a dialogue that I recently had with my heart. The italics are "me." The regular type is "my heart."

What do I need to stop thinking? That you're not special. That you have to know all the answers. *You mean, I don't.* That's right. That's how you sabotage yourself, thinking you have to be perfect all the time. You're always thinking that you have to do it differently—then you can't experience the joy and power you have within.

How can I remember not to sabotage myself? The key is to become aware when you're doing it and just stop. Feel what your body feels like when you do it. It recoils, and you feel sour inside. Then stop.

What do I need to know? Know that you have everything within you that you need to know. You don't need anyone. *But I want to have people in my life, relationships . . . I don't want to be all alone.* That's very different than needing. Needing reflects a lack of trust with yourself. The other way is being open to what the Universe brings you, and allows you to see that you are never alone because you hold the entire Universe within.

Your Prayer of Intention

Your *Prayer of Intention* represents three steps you will take during the following week to incorporate what you've learned in each chapter.

Example:

Three steps that I will take this week to help me connect with the voice of my heart are

1. I will meditate once a day

2. I will reflect on what stops me from believing that my higher self is my true self.

3. I will buy myself a gift.

My Heart Knows Affirmations

A good way to begin this potent exercise is to say, either aloud or silently, "My heart knows"; then complete the sentence with whatever arises for you. If the statement "feels right"—if you know it's right without knowing how you know—it is a message from your heart. As you practice, you'll be amazed by the messages your heart will reveal. As you work with this book, it will become easier and easier to hear your heart's messages.

Example:

"My heart knows *that it's right for me to meet Lisa tonight for dinner.*"

"My heart knows *that's it's better for me to spend the night at home.*"

Example:

" My heart knows *that I'm worthy of having a loving relationship.*"

"My heart knows *that I am a daughter of God.*"

Example:

" My heart knows that *I want to trust its messages, that they are my truth*."

"My heart knows *that even though I think I want that second donut, I really don't*."

Endnotes

Chapter One

"I was . . . held close in the arms of [someone] who had come to reveal all things to me." Helen Keller, *The Story of My Life* (New York: Bantam Books, 1990), 35.

"I read and walked for miles at night along the beach, writing bad blank verse and searching endlessly for someone who would step out of the darkness and change my life," novelist Anna Quindlen confessed. "It never crossed my mind that that person could be me." Anna Quindlen, *Living Out Loud* (New York: Random House, 1988), 11.

. . . We're wired neurologically as receivers, in tune with the nuances of voice, expression, sight, and sound, which register in our bodies as feelings and sensations . . . For more on this concept, see Joan Borysenko's *A Woman's Journey to God: Finding the Feminine Path* (New York: Riverhead Books/Penguin Putnam, 1999), 84.

"Our task is to heal the internal split that tells us to override [our] feelings, and intuition . . . and have the courage to . . . listen to our inner wisdom." Maureen Murdock, *The Heroine's Journey: A Woman's Quest for Wholeness* (Boston: Shambhala Publications, 1990), 25.

Chapter Two

The Family of Women encourages women to empower their own lives by supporting them to reclaim responsibility for their relationships. For more information, go to www.familyofwomen.org.

Chapter Five

"[In] the . . . spirit of woman's spirituality," author Joan Borysenko tells us, "every woman is a priestess." *A Woman's Journey to God: Finding the Feminine Path* (New York: Riverhead Books/Penguin Putnam, 1999), 243–244.

Chapter Seven

"No one is hurt by doing the right thing," says a Hawaiian proverb. Reynold Feldman, *World Treasury of Wisdom* (New York: HarperCollins, 1992), 68.

Chapter Eight

The inspiration for this chapter and much of the information about the Nine Muses was taken from Angeles Arrien, *The Second Half of Life: The Blossoming of Your Creative Self* (Boulder, Colorado: Sounds True Publishing, 1998), Audiotape #5. The information about the weeping statue was taken from Deepak Chopra, *SynchroDestiny: Discover the Power of Meaningful Coincidence to Manifest Abundance in Your Life* (Niles, Illinois: Nightingale-Conant, 1998), Audiotape 8A, Session 15.

Chapter Nine

Information about the Celtic belief that humans are made of clay and come from the underworld or world of Spirit, etc., was taken from John O'Donohue, *Anam Cara, Wisdom from the Celtic World* (Boulder, Colorado: Sounds True Publishing, 1996), Audiotape #3.

Chapter Ten

Information about the Celtic tradition of "soul partners" was taken from John O'Donohue, *Anam Cara, Wisdom from the Celtic World* (Boulder, Colorado: Sounds True Publishing, 1996), Audiotape #3. The information about mystical love and marriage according to the Jewish tradition was given to me by Jewish scholar and dear friend, Natalie Reid.

Selected Bibliography and Reading List

Now for some [additional] heartwork.

—Rainer Maria Rilke

The following books have been inspirational in the writing of this book and in helping me explore my divinity.

Arrien, Angeles. *The Four-Fold Way: Walking the Paths of the Warrior, Teacher, Healer, and Visionary.* San Francisco: HarperSanFrancisco, 1993.

Ban Breathnach, Sarah. *Something More: Excavating Your Authentic Self.* New York: Warner Books, 1998.

Biziou, Barbara. *The Joy of Ritual: Spiritual Recipes to Celebrate Milestones, Ease Transitions, and Make Every Day Sacred.* New York: Golden Books, 1999.

Borysenko, Joan. *A Woman's Journey to God: Finding the Feminine Path.* New York: Riverhead Books/Penguin Putnam, 1999.

Cameron, Julia. *Blessings: Prayers and Declarations for a Heartful Life.* New York: Jeremy P. Tarcher/Penguin Putnam, 1998.

Cameron, Julia. *Heart Steps: Prayers and Declarations for a Creative Life*. New York: Jeremy P. Tarcher/Penguin Putnam, 1997.

Chopra, Deepak. *SynchroDestiny: Discover the Power of Meaningful Coincidence to Manifest Abundance in Your Life*. Niles, Illinois: Nightingale-Conant, 1998. Audiotape.

Gatusso, Joan. *A Course in Life: The Twelve Universal Principles for Achieving a Life Beyond Your Dreams*. New York: Jeremy P. Tarcher/Penguin Putnam, 1998.

Gawain, Shakti. *Meditations: Creative Visualization and Meditation Exercises to Enrich Your Life*. San Rafael, California: New World Library, 1991.

Jaidar, George. *The Soul: An Owner's Manual—Discovering the Life of Fullness*. New York: Paragon House, 1995.

Keller, Helen. *The Story of My Life*. New York: Bantam Books, 1990.

Lamott, Anne. *Traveling Mercies: Some Thoughts on Faith*. New York: Pantheon Books/Random House, 1999.

Levoy, Gregg, *Callings: Finding and Following an Authentic Life*. New York: Random House, 1997

Maggio, Rosalie, ed. *The New Beacon Book of Quotations by Women*. Boston: Beacon Press, 1996.

Murdock, Maureen. *The Heroine's Journey: A Woman's Quest for Wholeness*. Boston: Shambhala Publications, 1990.

Myss, Caroline. *Anatomy of the Spirit: The Seven Stages of Power and Healing*. New York: Harmony Books/Crown Publishers, 1996.

Naparstek, Belleruth. *Staying Well with Guided Imagery: How to Harness the Power of Your Imagination for Health and Healing*. New York: Warner Books, 1994.

O'Donohue, John. *Anam Cara, A Book of Celtic Wisdom*. New York: Cliff Street Books/HarperCollins, 1997.

O'Donohue, John. *Eternal Echoes: Celtic Reflections on Our Yearning to Belong*. New York: Cliff Street Books/HarperCollins, 1999.

Quinn, Janet F. *I Am a Woman Finding My Voice: Celebrating the Extraordinary Blessings of Being a Woman*. New York: Eagle Brook/William Morrow, 1999.

Remen, Rachel Naomi. *Kitchen Table Wisdom: Stories That Heal*. New York: Riverhead Books/Penguin Putnam, 1997.

Remen, Rachel Naomi. *My Grandfather's Blessings: Stories of Strength, Refuge, and Belonging*. New York: Riverhead Books/Penguin Putnam, 2000.

Small, Jacquelyn. *Becoming a Practical Mystic: Creating Purpose for Our Spiritual Future*. Wheaton, Illinois: Quest Books, 1998.

Telesco, Patricia. *365 Goddess: A Daily Guide to the Magic and Inspiration of the Goddess*. San Francisco: HarperSanFrancisco, 1998.

Vanzant, Iyanla. *One Day My Soul Just Opened Up, 40 Days and 40 Nights Toward Spiritual Strength and Personal Growth*. New York: Fireside/Simon & Schuster, 1998.

Virtue, Doreen. *Divine Guidance: How to Have a Dialogue with God and Your Guardian Angels*. Los Angeles: Renaissance Books, 1998.

Waldherr, Kris. *Embracing the Goddess Within: A Creative Guide for Women*. Hillsboro, Oregon: Beyond Words Publishing, 1997.

Williamson, Marianne. *Enchanted Love: The Mystical Power of Intimate Relationships*. New York: Simon & Schuster, 1999.

Williamson, Marianne. *A Woman's Worth*. New York: Ballantine Books, 1993.

Zukav, Gary. *Soul Stories*. New York: Simon & Schuster, 2000.

Acknowledgments

My heart goes out to so many. To Natalie Reid, dear friend and first editor of this manuscript, who helped transform some of my ideas and my writing into a respectable book, my unending appreciation. I'd like to express my gratitude to Mira Furth, kindred spirit and "priestess," who co-led the pilot *Your Heart Knows* workshops with me, and who also blessed this manuscript with un-altering love and support.

Thanks to Anne and Josef Kottler for providing me with the opportunity to consult with them on so many wonderful writing projects that contributed invaluable information and inspired me in the writing of this book, and for leading me to my agent, Barbara Neighbors Deal. I deeply appreciate the New England branch of the Family of Women, for providing me with the arena, love, and support that allowed me to experiment with concepts for the book, particularly those women with whom I participated in the Leadership Training Program, who were my guinea pigs for the development of the *Rose Petal* Ceremony.

Blessings to all the women who shared their stories with me about what their hearts know, including those women who attended the pilot *Your Heart Knows* workshops, and those from the "Westboro Ladies Night Out," whose input contributed to the writing of the *Loving Body* Ceremony. And special thanks to Mary Lynn Hackett, whose flexibility, dedication, and care for my son while I was completing this manuscript put me at such ease, that I was able to complete it without a care in the world.

I wish to express my heartfelt thanks to Karen Bouris, Publisher of Inner Ocean Publishing, for seeing the value and beauty in this work, even though when she first read the manuscript some of the "pieces of the puzzle" were in the wrong place. Karen's genuine openness and stance regarding the author-publisher relationship is truly awesome and can serve as a model for the entire publishing industry. Blessings to Heather McArthur, my editor at Inner Ocean, who inspired me to fit the pieces of the puzzle where they belong. Heather was truly the midwife of this book, helping it give birth to the perfection it calls its own. Heather is a pro, and so open, too. Special thanks to Associate Editor, Alma Bune, for seeing to it that I began my relationship with Inner Ocean Publishing with an exotic "taste of Maui," which remains faithfully (and beautifully) on my kitchen table, and for all the "behind the scenes" work that she contributed toward the publication of this book. To Mark Kerr, for his devotion and sales and marketing expertise, and Katie McMillian, for all her efforts in helping to publicize the book, I offer my kindest thanks.

My heart is a bottomless pit of love and appreciation for Barbara Neighbors Deal of Literary Associates, who is so much more to me than just my literary agent. Spiritual companion and friend, Barbara has been the conduit of so many things sacred for me, one being the publication of this book by Inner Ocean Publishing. She believed in me and in this project through thick and thin, and has stood by me, even when I had my doubts. Every author should know what it is like to have an agent like Barbara Deal.

I humbly express my gratitude to George Jaidar, guide of all guides (human, that is) without whom this book wouldn't be that which it is, because I wouldn't be aware of who I am. As I express this gratitude, I bow in reverence to the Cosmos, the Source, Creator of all things, for "the process of being," for my life—so full, my cup runneth over. I strive to emulate You always and in all ways.

Finally, I exude limitless love and gratitude to my husband, Bill, who blessed me with the opportunity to stay home and write, for his belief and trust in me, and in this book.

A Request from the Author:
Those Three Precious Little Words . . .

Thank you for reading *Your Heart Knows the Answer*. I hope that your time spent with this book has enabled you to *listen for* and to *live according to* what your heart knows in new and meaningful ways. I'd be delighted to hear that it has allowed you to *claim* your higher self as your true, authentic self.

Now, I ask you to consider the following:

Remember a time in your life, perhaps during your teens, when you wanted to be in love *so* much that you dreamed about having those "three little words" whispered in your ear?

"I love you."

You imagined that *then* everything would work out just right.

How many relationships did it take for you to realize that those words meant little, unless you first loved yourself? Why didn't anybody ever encourage us to cling to the words *"My heart knows,"* so that we could discover the meaning of *self-love*? Our lives might have been very different.

My vision for writing this book, as well as for future *Your Heart Knows* books, is to bring the meaning of the words *"My heart knows"* to women everywhere. I want to help women say, *"My heart knows,"* knowing that these words really mean, "I love myself."

155

You can help spread the "your heart knows" message. If you'd like to share a story about something that you've learned from working with this book, I'd love to include it as inspiration in an upcoming book.

Please send your story about a time in your life when you listened to what your heart knew and the gifts you received as a result. Or, if you knew something in your heart, yet didn't listen, tell me about one of those times (we've all had them), the lessons you learned, and what you discovered about yourself.

If you'd like to share a "heart" quote that you've come across that has special meaning for you, or one you wrote, please send this as well.

We're all more alike than you may think. Your personal sharing can help readers who may find themselves in a similar situation to recognize the voice of their hearts and to follow its wisdom. Please send your own *Your Heart Knows* stories to the address below. Or submit them at www.yourheartknows.com.

Your Heart Knows Stories
P.O. Box 994
Westboro, MA 01581-9998

Thank you very much. I look forward to hearing from you.

With love,
Gail Harris

About the Author

Gail Harris's writing—whether an article, an advertising campaign, or a book—celebrates getting to the heart of the matter. An award-winning copywriter, she has developed advertising materials for a wide range of companies, including Avon, *Yoga Journal*, the Omega Institute for Holistic Studies, and Sounds True Publishing. For two years, she lived and worked at the Kripalu Center for Yoga and Health, in Lenox, Massachusetts, where she studied yoga and meditation.

Besides joyfully raising her son, writing, and leading *Your Heart Knows* workshops, she currently volunteers her time with Resolve, the national infertility organization. She invites you to correspond with her and visit **www.yourheartknows.com** to download an audio version of the *Loving Body* Affirmation, the *Mystical Romance* Meditation, and the *Fields of Now* Meditation.

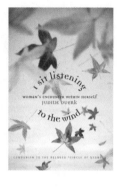
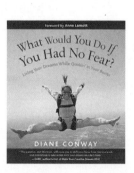